# TABLE OF CONTENTS

WHY I WROTE THIS GUIDE

THE HISTORY OF REAL ESTATE IN NYC

TERMS YOU SHOULD KNOW

REAL ESTATE AGENCIES AND HOW THEY WORK

SHOULD YOU USE AN AGENT?

HOW TO PICK A REAL ESTATE AGENT AND MAXIMIZE YOUR RELATIONSHIP WITH THEM

REAL ESTATE ATTORNEYS: YES, YOU SHOULD HAVE ONE-WHAT THEY DO FOR YOU AND HOW TO PICK ONE

WHAT'S IN A REAL ESTATE CONTRACT? : WHAT AM I AGREEING TO?

YOUR CLOSING – WHAT TO BRING – WHAT TO EXPECT

CLOSING COSTS

THE APPRAISAL – WHAT IS THE PROCESS AND WHAT IF, GOD FORBID, IT COMES IN LOW?

FOR SELLERS: WHAT'S IN AN EXCLUSIVE CONTRACT WITH A REAL ESTATE AGENCY?

FOR SELLERS: HOW TO PRICE YOUR PROPERTY?

FOR SELLERS: BEFORE YOU SELL –

RENOVATION AND REPAIRS

FOR SELLERS: BEFORE YOU SELL - DETAILS YOUR AGENT NEEDS TO KNOW

FOR SELLERS: BEFORE YOU SELL – STAGING AND PLANNING TO SHOW

FOR SELLERS: OFFERS

FOR BUYERS: BEFORE YOU START LOOKING

FOR BUYERS: BOROUGHS AND NEIGHBORHOODS

FOR BUYERS: WHERE TO LOOK FOR LISTINGS IN NYC

FOR BUYERS: STEPS TO PURCHASING

FOR BUYERS: CO-OPS VS CONDOS

FOR BUYERS: GETTING A LOAN

**FOR BUYERS: HOW TO DECIDE HOW MUCH TO OFFER AND HOW HIGH TO GO**

**FOR BUYERS: SETTLING IN**

# WHY I WROTE THIS GUIDE:

The NYC real estate market is changing. More women, people of color, first generation Americans, international buyers, and individuals who did not come from affluence, have discovered that owning property in NYC can be lucrative, rewarding and, perhaps, attainable. Because of this shift away from family chains of NYC real estate ownership, more people entering the market don't necessarily have expert counsel from close relatives or friends who understand the details, risks, and range of possible benefits of a standard real estate transaction from their own experience.

It's not that I think life can be fair, but I think everyone can benefit from solid, NYC specific, current, honest, information. Maybe this will level the playing field a little- perhaps making it possible for more people who had never thought of themselves as NYC homeowners, or investors, to benefit from the joys of owning (or making a profit by selling) property in New York City—without having every possible advantage in life or the heart of a miser.

Meanwhile, despite the ongoing recession, or maybe because of it, Millennials, even single ones, (real estate used to be a couple's game) have discovered that owning property in nyc can be a prudent investment. But whatever wisdom there may be in owning a home in New York does not prevent the anxiety of having a huge percentage of your money (and often your family's money) at stake.

Furthermore, the activity of buying and selling real estate in nyc is uniquely complicated. The role of the real estate agent/broker in New York City, unlike other places, is limited to the non-legal parts of the deal. In most states the agent can write, change, and interpret contracts and has access to all materials pertinent to the purchase or sale which means that in other places buyers and sellers have one point of contact for the things that affect their sale most.

Buyers and sellers in NYC however, are obliged to retain a real estate attorney even if they are using an agent, plus, if they are seeking financing, they often need the services of a mortgage broker or banker who comes with their own set of critical, proprietary, information. The offshoot of this is that important details about a sale are spread out between three individuals, who may, or may not, be communicating with each other effectively.

Also, because typically the attorney is only able to gather information once a contract arrives in their office -- many significant details about a property are unknown to the buyer until after a price has been negotiated and an agreement has been made - an order that is, of course, totally ass backwards in terms of making good decisions or negotiating effectively from the beginning, and can result in aggravation for both sellers and buyers as terms are sometimes renegotiated or contracts abandoned entirely once all the facts are known.

Despite how limited my power as an nyc real estate broker may be, beyond the negotiation of price, and facilitating visits or showings of apartments-- clients rely heavily on me as their primary contact. At such a critical time, people want all their information to come from one cohesive and trustworthy source -- and that's me--their agent. I have experience, am able to explain stuff, and I'm a pretty nice person. Most customers and clients have lots of questions that deserve good answers. They're not casual questions either. They are middle-of-the-night, drenched-in-sweat, should-I-or-shouldn't-I, questions that naturally occur as they consider the radical impact that the movement of such a large amount of money will have on their life.

The new world of buyers and sellers are a naturally skeptical group—they like objectivity and facts, so they can make their own informed decisions. They are data savvy and accustomed to having access to detailed information in order to make a decision. They are also, overall, fairly mistrustful of real estate agents. Perhaps for good reason. Real estate agents are ranked very low, next to attorneys, in terms of perception of trustworthiness.

It is obvious to anyone that if a broker is paid by commission (and is only paid once an apartment sells) the agent's self-interest is not always the same as the interest of their clients – which no matter how many times salespeople insist doesn't matter and that they really only care about their customers – is nonsense, unless human nature is somehow irrelevant in real estate. And of course, it isn't. From the inside, I have of course, seen many shenanigans on the part of real estate agents that were not in the best interest of customers at all. Real estate is neither the cesspool some people imagine but it's not Eagle Scouts either.

For these reasons and many others (efficiency, preparedness before entering the real estate market, answering important questions customers might not know to ask, or that an agent might forget to mention once the break-neck speed of a NYC transaction begins) you would think there would be tons of current reference books on the subject of buying and selling real estate in New York City—but there aren't. There are none that are comprehensive or even claim to be. Literally not one that is currently in print.

There is though one very good guide, published originally in 2003, with a 2013 4$^{th}$ edition called The Ultimate Guide To Buying and Selling Co-ops and Condos in NYC by J. Binder –the original published in 2003 with the 2013 edition only available used and selling for $900-1,000. Sure there are tell-all real estate books about the glamorous life of nyc brokers, and books about co-ops specifically, books about real estate overall, which are mostly irrelevant to New York City, and a tiny handful of much older, but very lightweight books about real estate in nyc, but things have changed since the 80s and it is a topic that, I, and most participants, feel, deserves a more thorough treatment.

I want to write this book… not so much because of my love of nyc real estate, or admiration of the real estate industry –but because I am fascinated by the incredible complexity of a New York City transaction and conscious of how many unique details are involved that can make a world of difference to a buyer or seller that can't be surmised without the real world experience that I have had in the industry. I want to offer a guide to NYC real estate that protects and informs participants entering or reentering the market, that helps them sleep a little better at night.

"Only a life lived for others is a life worthwhile"
- Albert Einstein

To everyone who doesn't own real estate in NYC but should

and also my adult kids Nathan and Sabina who remind me every day why I need to work.

Copyright © 2023 Alexandra Florio
All rights reserved.

# THE HISTORY OF REAL ESTATE IN NYC

From the first transaction by the Dutch West India company with the Lenape natives of New York - the history of New York City real estate has been a complex story full of scandal, intrigue, and trickery, all wrapped in troubling, but exciting, cut-throat competition (sometimes literally). If you want evidence that life isn't fair you need only look at the purchase and sale of property within the city of New York.

There are many versions of what might have happened when Peter Minuit of the Dutch East India Company arrived in Manhattan. Records of the transaction are scant and the only details we are sure about are that the Dutch believed that what they had bargained for was ownership of the Island of Manhattan and that it cost them very little. The purchase seems to have been made in exchange for a small supply of tools useful for making wampum, the recognized currency for the Lenape.

One small catch though, was that in most accounts, the Lenape were divided into several sub-groups, and it is entirely possible that the Lenape occupying the majority of the island, were never consulted about the trade, suggested by their repeated attempts to kill all subsequent Dutch settlers. Alternatively, there is also some evidence suggesting that what the Lenape thought they were selling may have only been hunting rights, and not ownership. It is also reasonable to imagine that the Lenape realized immediately that the Dutch had resources, military and otherwise, that were far greater than theirs, and that the deal was made in an attempt to avoid colonization.

There was limited European development in New York City between the 1650s and the early 19$^{th}$ century but New York's position as a globally significant city was really sealed in the 1800s. This period saw rapid growth across the United States with Manhattan showing the highest increases in the nation, because of its readily accessible natural harbor on the East Coast. It was a convenient place to both receive immigrants and transfer imports and exports.

By the end of the 1800s, hundreds of thousands of immigrants poured into the country, the vast majority through the New York Harbor. Between 1800 and 1900 the population of New York increased by 50 times to roughly 3.4 million, more than double that of Chicago, the next largest city, at 1.7 million. Rapid industrialization, coupled with greater efficiency in agriculture, moved jobs from farms to cities. In 1800, 90 percent of the US labor force worked in agriculture, whereas by 1890 only 50 percent remained in agricultural trades.

The completion of The Erie Canal in the 1820s linked the Hudson River to Lake Erie facilitating trade with the Midwest and established New York City as the most significant industrial stronghold on the East Coast. Manhattan's position as commercial capital was further strengthened a decade later in the 1830s by train lines built just a few blocks east of the Hudson shoreline, linking downtown Manhattan to the Midwest, making New York an ideal place for international trade to and from Europe.

Also, by the mid 1800s industrialists enjoyed the development of steel frame construction for building and the invention of the elevator--which, together, made multi-floor buildings possible. Stacked floor buildings were ideal for running steam-engine based factories which needed to be connected by pipes and for housing dense populations of workers. The architectural innovations also facilitated the construction of skyscrapers in the 1920s across the city as industrial jobs began to give way to white collar ones.

The end of the Civil War in 1865 brought the movement of African Americans to northern cities and conscious segregation started immediately. As people of color arrived in certain neigborhoods of NYC, the European American residents of those places, began to move out, heading to parts of the city where opportunities were no better – with no greater incentive than seeking separation.

Demand for NYC real estate rose rapidly after the Civil War and it is reported that prices along Park Avenue increased by 44% between 1885 and 1929. However, they plummeted again during the depression, and didn't recover to pre 1930s levels, for many decades.

At the same time the 1930s saw a steep rise in the cost of rent, often outpacing wages, as movement to cities continued throughout the depression. Urban environments offered greater job opportunity despite widespread unemployment nationally. In addition, because New York operated a robust subway system, for people who couldn't afford housing convenient to their job, subway commuting was possible. Much rental housing at this time was overcrowded and poorly cared for by landlords.

Prices remained fairly stable throughout the second world war, giving way to a housing boom, with increased sales prices and rents, when soldiers returned home. This demand though was somewhat offset by the construction of interstate highways at this time allowing for the creation of suburban housing serving NYC.

After the war, low interest rate mortgages were made available, to select veterans, through the 1944 G.I. Bill of Rights. For those deemed eligible, the bill provided cash stipends for schooling, low-interest mortgages, job skills training, low-interest business loans, and unemployment benefits. Distribution of funds was left to local governments, and decided by committee, giving these groups leeway to entertain their own prejudices in determining who would make "best use" of the benefit. This overwhelmingly excluded veterans of color, and because low interest lending was still subject to approval by banks, who frequently refused to lend to non-white applicants, or to people without prior credit -- the actual GI pay-out was heavily skewed in favor of people of European American decent and greater privilege prior to their service.

This began a several decade long pattern of people able to qualify for home loans, generally the more affluent, being tempted away from the urban center by the promise of a two car garage and racially segregated existence, leaving urban resources, like schools, housing, and hospitals, with precarious support.

Meanwhile, developers and real estate agents, bragged and advertised that they were building enclaves of "the right kind of people" in suburban communities, as one affluent NYC suburb vied to outdo the other as the most "exclusive". This rhetoric, of course, left many with the feeling that the urban center of the city was where "the wrong kind of people" had been left behind, and indeed, the declining affluence of the tax base combined with a growing population of job seekers, met by a lack of responsiveness by the state and federal government, NYC began to struggle.

Large numbers of workers coming into New York City after WWII, often never really finding the opportunity they had hoped for, continued throughout the 1970s. As manufacturing jobs disappeared by over a million from 1945-1965, the strain of needed public programs, without adequate tax funding from the state or federal government, worsened and New York City headed into a steady decline. By the 1970s NYC had acquired over 5 bn of short term debt with essentially no ability to repay it, leaving the city unable to borrow any more, despite great need. It was considered too great a risk. Meanwhile prices doubled from the 50s to the 60s, and then nearly doubled again, from the 60s through the 70s.

In 1975 New York requested that the federal government back its bonds, as it made sweeping cuts, in an attempt to bring the city back from poverty. In response to this request President Ford heartily, and publicly, refused the plea with such gusto and showmanship, it made headlines suggesting what may have been an attempt to impress the rest of the nation with his callous bravado towards the City of New York.

This public demonstration of contempt for NYC, illustrated an increasingly national fear and disregard for the plight of the crime-ridden, welfare strained, city and did not hide an implication that problems unique to NYC were due to some kind of moral failing in its inhabitants, instead of the unique hardship of density and rapid growth, an accusation that has been echoed many times since about urban centers throughout the country.

After waves of massive cuts among city workers, in an attempt to manage NYCs spiraling costs and anguished protests of those cuts, it was ultimately the city workers' unions themselves that, with NYC on the brink of bankruptcy, essentially saved the city. City workers' unions agreed to offer their pensions as backing for NYC bonds. This unique act of compassion coupled with vocal suggestions from abroad that a bankrupt New York would throw the value of the U.S. dollar as into question, compelled the previously hard-hearted Ford to find support for a 2.5 billion per year assist for New York until it had stabilized again.

As New York City lifted out of bankruptcy in the late 70s, international buyers began to enter the market. As the economy improved after two early 1980s recessions, NYC prices rose rapidly by nearly six times in the mid to late 80s, and more than doubled again in the 90s (though the *volume* of home sales declined in the face of high 18 plus percent interest rates). This period—the mid 80s to the early 1990s were notable for the combination of a robust economy, a unique popular thirst for luxury urban living fueled by the booming financial industry, plus availability of a variety of 'creative financing' solutions for buyers seeking to purchase. The trend towards over-the-top conspicuous spending during the pre- 'pimp my crib' era, plus lower cost international travel, attracted, more and more foreign investors to a very glamourous NYC.

The destruction of the World Trade Center in 2001 inspired an a brief decline in housing demand in the downtown areas surrounding the World Trade Center and spurred a drop in international investment. This movement away from downtown areas, though, created renewed interest in midtown, long considered commercial-only, as a place to live continuing to this day.

Downtown sales, however, rebounded fast, and even just a year later, in 2002, had returned to nearly pre 9/11 levels. This local recovery though was followed soon after by an unprecedented national housing crisis in 2008 anchored by Lehman Brothers filing for bankruptcy amidst a national recession. Apt prices in NYC fell as much as 20% in some sectors, finding their lowest point in 2011. The decline in value was disproportionate between NYC neighborhoods, some faring better than others. Over the course of the next ten years, NYC prices rebounded consistently and rapidly, significantly outpacing the national average. By 2016 housing prices in Manhattan had fully recovered and all-time record high sales prices were recorded throughout Manhattan and increased by 30% since 2008 across the board.

Despite uniquely low interest rates, more recently, NYC saw a slight decline again, from 2017 to 2019 in some combination of what looks like a natural correction, an oversupply of higher priced new construction and luxury units, plus a federal tax bill that decreased interest deductibility across the board.

Then COVID. The years following 2020 saw movement out of large cities, including New York, especially among the affluent, into areas that offered more comfortable social distancing, creating an oversupply of available properties, with very few buyers. However, despite all dramatic warnings that this would be 'the end of NYC' as soon as some restrictions were lifted – the sales volume in 2021 was the highest in over 3 years in part due to extraordinarily low interest rates and pent-up pandemic demand. This created a bubble that did though burst very quickly as interest rates rose to 7% from 3% and transaction volume declined by 24% again in late 2022 but it was certainly a pretty clear indication of the endurance of NYC.

Now is a fascinating time in New York. Rising interest rates create an environment, for now, where it is my belief that seller price expectations may not have caught up to buyer reality—but I believe they will. Plus, the fast movement into and out of the city has slowed to pre-pandemic levels, so the urgency on the part of buyers and sellers has subsided. There is a feeling of waiting and watching as buyers and sellers try to determine both potential shifts in the economy and their own long-term plans. The worst of the pandemic may be over but the world has been changed by it and people are evaluating their housing and lifestyle options.

I have recently heard more than one prospective seller say that they want to sell but are busy figuring out how a move would affect their life. The pandemic shifted the framework of how people perceive their work and life and what would satisfy them in a place to live. New York City offers so many unique opportunities, economic and otherwise, as it always has, that even as it restructures, I believe it will always be a valuable place for some of the nation's most ambitious and talented to congregate and dream. This combination of history, charm and optimism, I believe, more than any specific economic detail is what has kept, and will continue to keep, prices high, and rising, long into the future.

# TERMS YOU SHOULD KNOW

Some guidance here… I have kept this list short on purpose and used the most colloquial, most NYC specific, versions of these terms. I would advise just reading though this list so that if they come up during some part of your transaction – they are not entirely unfamiliar. Alternately you might use it for reference, but it is likely not comprehensive enough to answer every question. NYC real estate is the ultimate expression of "you don't know what you don't know" until you are standing right in the middle of confusion, generally with a lot of time pressure, so you might want to at least skim this list upfront.

Your broker, attorney, and mortgage professional should be able to fill in any blanks in your understanding of terms. Do not be shy about asking your team any questions you might have, and if they cannot answer your questions, you understand just keep asking.

A

**Adjustable Rate Mortgage**

A term loan with rates that may fluctuate from year to year based on interest rates. Some loans offer a fixed rate for a given term after which rates become adjustable.

**Accepted Offer**

An act of the property owner agreeing to and accepting the offer and terms of the purchaser. It can be either verbal or written but is not legally bound.

## Air Rights

The right to use, develop or otherwise control the space above a property. Air Rights can be sold, rented or leased to another party.

## Alcove Studio

A one-room apartment with a separate sleeping area.

## Amenities

Features or facilities of an individual apartment/unit/building. E.g. gym, storage, bike room, common space.

## Appraisal

An assessment of the value of a property. After contract signing a lender will send an independent appraiser who will assess the value of the property based on comps in order to determine that its perceived value justifies the amount of the loan requested. This assessment – if it does not equal the contract price of the unit - can be contested.

## B

## Broker/Associate Broker/Salesperson

A state-licensed sales professional who acts as an agent for property owners, prospective purchasers, tenants and landlords in real estate transactions. You will hear the term *associate broker* which is the title for an agent who has obtained a broker's license who works as an independent contractor within an agency (the majority of brokers in NYC have this status. Very few NYC brokers work independently for a variety of good reasons) Alternatively, you will see the title *salesperson* This is the initial level of licensing by the state. To obtain a ***broker's license*** you must first hold a *salesperson's license* and complete a certain number of transactions before being allowed to take the broker's licensing exam. Some agents who meet the criteria for a broker's license just never bother taking the secondary exam and paying the additional fees associated with the title.

## Brownstone

A 19th century townhouse faced with brown sandstone.

# C

## Certificate of Occupancy (C of O)

Each New York City building is required to have a Certificate of Occupancy, a document indicating the structure is suitable for occupancy. This means that the building is in compliance with health and building codes. No one may legally occupy a building until the Department of Buildings has issued a CO.

## Classic Six

Found in pre-war buildings (see below), these six-room apartments feature two bedrooms, a dining room, living room, kitchen and a small maid's room.

## Closing

The final step in executing a real estate transaction. Closing is the transfer of ownership of a property from the seller to the buyer as per the sales contract. Generally, the closing takes place in the seller's attorney's office and is scheduled after all board interviews and financing is in place. Arranging a time for the closing may take several weeks because there are many parties involved. Closings may also be virtual but in-person closings are still more common.

## Closing Costs

Expenses incurred in a sale/purchase and paid at the time of closing — includes lawyer fees, taxes, and title insurance.

## Co-Broking

The practice of sharing the commission between the selling real estate broker or salesperson and the buyer's agent. Most, but not all, agents will co-broke.

## Combined Apartment

When an apartment is comprised of the combination of two adjoining apartments into one. Can be either side by side, to create a larger unit, or up and down to form a duplex or triplex.

## Commission

Payment to the buying or selling agent for his or her efforts in marketing, selling, or locating and negotiating a real estate property. Agreed upon at the time of the listing, the commission is usually expressed as a percentage of the total purchase price. Commissions typically range from **4% to 6% with 6% being most common.** The commission is typically paid by the seller and shared 50/50 with the buyers' agent.

Smaller agencies will sometimes charge the lower end of the commission range, but generally offer less exposure for a listing and may be more reluctant to co-broke a property- which limits the number of prospective buyers. Plus, lower commission may equal lower incentive for a buyer's agent to bring customers to a listing. Most major agency brokers will expect 5%-6%. It is common for 'better' brokers to hold firm at 6%- because they can, and because they anticipate more time and money involved in their marketing efforts.

## Commitment Letter

The final document issued by the lender guaranteeing the loan with specific terms, once any *'contingencies'* are met.

## Common Area

The area within a building that is available for use to all owners, tenants, and their invitees.

## Common Charges

Money owed monthly to maintain the common elements of a *condominium unit*. This number generally does NOT include property taxes. When talking about monthly charges for a condominium the property tax is generally noted separately.

## Comparables (or Comps), or CMA (Comparable Market Analysis)

*Comparables* refer to sold or currently on the market properties that are deemed similar to a subject property in size, condition, location, and amenities. Used in evaluating or establishing the fair market value of a property. A CMA is the analysis of several comparable properties.

## Condominium (Condo)

A building where individuals or parties own their unit outright (including individual utilities sometimes), but share common areas with the other unit owners in the building. A more liberal type of ownership than Cooperatives, Condominiums have more lenient subletting policies, typically less purchasing restrictions, often lower common charges than co-ops but also generally cost more per square foot than comparable co-ops. There are far fewer condos in NYC than co-ops and they are more typical in newer developments.

## Contract of Sale

A legally binding agreement between the buyer and seller. It is generally anchored by a 10% deposit by the purchaser placed until the closing into the selling attorneys escrow account. It is signed first by the buyer and then afterwards by the seller. It is not legally binding to either party until both parties have signed.

## Convertible Apartment

An apartment that can be renovated to create an additional bedroom or reconfigured in some other way. Terms like "a convertible two" refers to a one bedroom apartment that can be converted to a two bedroom. Review the requirements for the creation of a legal bedroom in NYC before presuming this is realistically possible.

## Contingencies

Actions which must be completed in a certain way in order to meet the requirements of a contract or agreement. Some more common contingencies in a sales contract include a *'finance contingency'*, requiring that in order for the buyer to be obligated to complete the purchase they must be able to obtain the specified amount of financing. Rarely a buyer can request an 'inspection contingency', suggesting that the buyer will have the right to be released from the contract in the event that an inspection comes back unsatisfactorily. Only a minority of buyers request inspections for co-ops, because the major expenses for upkeep are shared by all the owners, and generally if an inspection is required it is done before the contract is signed. *Finance contingencies* are much more common.

The same term is used to describe requirements of a mortgage 'commitment letter' that must be met in order to guarantee financing.

## Cooperative (Co-Op)

A well-established type of ownership of property common in NYC where the purchaser of an individual unit owns shares in the cooperative building (similar to shares in a corporation) that are allocated to the individual unit. The number of shares owned is determined by several factors including the size of the apartment.

The purchaser is buying stock in the building and receiving what is known as *a proprietary lease* that allows occupancy and use of the unit.

## D

**Deed**

A written document by which title of property is conveyed from one party to another.

**Duplex**

An apartment that occupies two levels connected by a private interior staircase.

## E

**Escrow**

A bond, deed, or other document kept in the custody of a third party, taking effect only when a specified condition has been fulfilled. This term comes up at contract signing when typically, 10 percent of the contract price is deposited into the selling attorneys escrow account—which will later be applied to the purchase at the closing. The amount collected at signing is generally 10% even if the percentage down for the loan amount will be greater. This amount is also known as an 'earnest money deposit'.

**Exclusive Listing or Exclusive Agreement**

A contract whereby the owner of a property grants only one agent (known as the *'listing agent'*) the right to market the property for sale for a certain period of time with the understanding that if the agreed upon asking price for the property is attained – the commission is earned - even if the seller chooses to decline the offer. The exclusive agent may, or may not, co-broke the property with an outside agent as agreed by the terms of the exclusive agreement.

## F

**Financing**

Borrowing funds to purchase a real property.

**Fixed-Rate Mortgage**

A loan where the interest rate remains constant over the entire term of the loan. The most common kind of mortgage. Generally, for a term of 15 or 30 years. The alternative being an *adjustable-rate mortgage.*

**Flip Tax**

Tax imposed on an individual cooperative apartment at the time of sale by the cooperative. Flip tax can either be paid by the seller or purchaser, subject to contract negotiations, and is usually expressed as a percentage of the purchase price. It is most typically paid by the seller.

**Full Bath**

A bathroom with a sink, toilet, bath, or a shower. All homes must have at least one full bath. The alternative is a *half bath or powder room* referring to a room with only a toilet and sink.

## G

**Grandfather Clause or 'Grandfathered'**

If a new, more restrictive, rule is passed those people whose activity was allowed under the previous law may be allowed to continue to enjoy the previous privilege.

## H

### Half Bath/Powder Room

A bathroom with a sink and toilet, but without a bath or a shower.

## J

### Junior 4

A one-bedroom with a large living room, or other space large enough to section off a small office or bedroom (note: In NYC, a bedroom must have a window).

## L

### Lien

A legal claim against property for money owed. Can interfere with a prospective sale. Most common example would be money owed to a contractor for work previously done.

### Listing/Listing Agreement

A 'Listing Agreement' also known as an 'exclusive agreement' is a contract enlisting a real estate professional to market a property. Available apartments, homes, or spaces, are also referred to as 'listings'.

### Loft

Open-plan living space that was converted from commercial space (oftentimes factories or warehouses) to residential space. Lofts traditionally have high ceilings, large windows and lots of open space, free of partitions.

## M

### Maintenance

Monthly charges paid by the owner of a unit within a **cooperative building** for their share of costs to maintain the common elements of the building. It includes the building's operating costs, real estate taxes, and debt on the building's underlying mortgage.

### Maisonette

An apartment on the first floor of a building that has a private entrance.

### Managing Agent or Management Company

An independent company or agent that is hired to manage a property on behalf and for the interest of its owner.

### Mansion Tax

A 1 percent tax on the selling price for any home costing more than $1 million.

### Mortgage

Money borrowed from a lender in order to purchase a property. Mortgages vary in terms of length and interest rates.

## N

### Negotiation

The process of discussing an issue between two parties aimed at reaching an agreement.

## O

## Offer

An expression of the desire to purchase a property at a specific price with specific terms. The terms specified at the time of offer typically include the amount that will be financed (if any), and any *contingencies* which might typically include whether or not an inspection is required *(inspection contingency)*, and whether or not the ability to attain financing is a requirement of the purchase *(finance contingency)*.

## Open House

A specified time when a property, that is being offered for sale, is available to be viewed by prospective buyers. Brokers advertise open houses to help the sale of a property.

## Open Listing

A listing where the owner of the property allows more than one broker to market a property and only pays commission to the one that provides the purchaser.

## P

## Penthouse

An apartment normally on the top floor of a high-rise building. Typically considered desirable and sometimes including additional amenities.

## Pied a Terre

A French term that refers to an apartment that is not the primary residence of the owner. A Pied a Terre is used when the property's owner lives in another location and uses the residence sporadically. Not all co-op buildings allow units to be used as pied a terres.

## Post-War

A post war building is one that was built after World War II. It can suggest slightly different construction details.

## Points

Fees paid by the borrower directly to the lender at closing, in exchange for a reduced interest rate. Each point is equal to 1% of the principal of the mortgage.

## Powder Room

Also known as a half bath.

## Pre-War

A pre-war building is one that was built before World War II. Pre-war apartments may have larger dimensions, higher ceilings, period details and hardwood floors.

## Property Tax

The levy on a property that the owner is required to pay. In condos it is calculated per unit in co-ops it is shared by the co-operative with the amount divided between units.

## Prospectus

A document with all information buyers need on a new condo (or building in the process of converting into a coop or condo); also referred to as the offering plan.

# R

## Reserve Fund

An account reserved to provide funds for future expenses in order to maintain the cooperative or condominium building. A larger reserve fund is an indicator of a healthy and stable piece of property, improving overall value for shareholders and prospective buyers.

## S

### Sale Price

Also known as the *'purchase price'* this is the amount of money paid by the purchaser to the seller of real property at closing.

### Shares

Shares represent the proportion of a co-operative building allocated to an individual unit based on the size and value of the apartment. It is represented as a specific number.

### Sponsor Unit

An apartment in a coop still owned by the original owner or corporation that turned the building from a rental into a coop. Sponsor units are often unrenovated, less expensive, and don't require board approval to buy.

### Sublet Policy

A co-operative building policy regulating the limits and requirements for owners wishing to rent out their unit to a subleasing tenant. In cooperative ownership, the owner of the unit (proprietary tenant) may only sublet pursuant to the rules of the building. A typical co-operative sublet policy might be two years **'owner occupancy'**(the owner must personally inhabit the unit) and then two years allowable subleasing after which the owner must return or sell.

## T

### Tax Abatement

A government-offered financial incentive, in which the owner of a new construction property and/or the developer **pays reduced** taxes for a certain amount of time — usually 10–15 years that is then passed on as an initial savings in taxes to the purchaser.

**Title**

The legal term for the evidence that the owner is in lawful possession of the land and property.

**Townhouse**

A townhouse is a low-rise private residential building where at least one wall is shared with another residence.

## U

**Unit**

A single residence within a building.

**Utilities**

Services such as water, gas, and electricity. Some utilities in some buildings are included in the maintenance charges.

## W

**Walk Up Building**

A building that does not have an elevator.

**Walk Through**

The inspection of a property immediately before the closing to ensure that the property does not have any new, post-contract, damage

# REAL ESTATE AGENCIES AND HOW THEY WORK

Real estate agencies can be a mystery to the public unless you have personally worked inside of one. Questions like how commissions are divided, what different titles mean, what constitutes co-broking, and how it could impact you, all affect the atmosphere of real estate in NYC.

**Real Estate Salesperson vs. Real Estate Broker**

Ah the great "Does obtaining a broker's license actually matter" debate. In most industries participants are economically rewarded for stepping up the certification ladder, but since real estate is entirely commission based, this is a place where it does not translate directly into greater economic success. Also, truth be told, as someone who has had a broker's license for a while, the majority of information on the broker's exam is not relevant to NYC at all. Lots to memorize about 'easements' or 'littoral rights' do nothing to enhance your knowledge of New York City sales. It is a statewide exam.

Plus, maintaining a broker's license is more expensive than just keeping the salespersons license. The rates paid to the state to get it, and maintain it, are higher than for the salespersons license. Dues for any kind of real estate organizations also tend to be higher for people with broker's licenses. Also, the intended purpose of it, I suppose, was mostly a way to distinguish who might have the expertise to legally operate their own independent real estate practice—or create an agency and have other people work under them. However, in NYC, virtually no one starts their own practice for a number of very good reasons (need too much legal representation – too much marketing to be competitive) and so even those of us with brokers licenses have the downgraded sounding title of *associate broker* within our agencies. We work under the umbrella of an assigned broker for the company that has hired us, even though we may have never met that person.

So having a broker's license vs a salespersons license is really only significant in that it requires 2-3 years' experience in real estate to apply plus the completion of a certain number of closed deals during that time equaling a certain number of points, an additional 75-hour licensing class with slightly more involved material than for the salespersons license and then passing a kind of challenging exam.

But is it game changing for practicing day to day real estate in NYC? Probably not. Maybe the broker licensing materials address investment properties a little more thoroughly and most people I know with broker's licenses seem to be a little more comfortable with investment sales but overall *salespeople* and *brokers* are pretty similar.

## Co-broking

These days most agencies readily co-broke all listings that they sell. That simply means that the selling agent will willingly allow agents from any other agency to bring (or send) their customers to see the apartment they are selling, will present offers coming from buyer's agents along with offers coming directly from buyers working without agents, and then, if the sale is made to a customer with a buyer's agent, share the commission 50/50 with the other agent.

It is safe to presume that all major NYC agencies will happily co-broke any listing. In fact there is an organization called REBNY (Real Estate Board of New York) that major agencies overwhelmingly belong to (with dues paid into it by agents typically) that requires it's members to officially agree to co-broke all listings without any shenanigans.

Smaller agencies though, especially in boroughs outside of Manhattan, occasionally do not belong to REBNY and are not obliged to co-broke listings, in which case, it makes sense to ask directly if they do. In some cases, they will not, on certain listings but will on others, or frustratingly, will say that they are willing to co-broke but will, in fact restrict access or downgrade offers that come from buyers with buying agents. This is uncommon, and less likely with higher price point listings.

When I work with buyers outside of Manhattan on lower price point purchases, I assure them that I will be able to tell from experience if a selling agent is avoiding me, or responding coolly to my presence. If I realize this is the case I promise to inform my buyer directly of this reality – and will remove myself officially from the transaction while continuing to counsel them on the sale with no expectation of commission, with the hope that they will refer me in the future. Yes, it sucks, but I know of no other way to address this frustrating, if rare, reality.

**Commission Splits, Leads, How Your Agent Gets Paid**

Typically, your real estate agent will share their commission with their agency in what is known as a 'split'. In many of the larger agency's splits can start at 50% and go up from there, generally depending on how much volume the agent closes in the previous year – getting above 50% requires a fair bit of sales volume equaling roughly what would be an income of $140K or higher for the agent – heavily incentivizing higher earnings (as if you weren't incentivized enough). In most agencies the majority of the money is made by a minority of agents—it is not uncommon for a lot of agents to be doing relatively poorly (and then typically quit) with several doing incredibly well (Million Dollar Agent ((though, truly a million dollar sale in NYC is not considered all that extraordinary)) while a number are doing just ok.

Large agencies also typically charge agents fees that range somewhat but are typically around $2500K a year referred to as 'legal fees' or 'administrative fees' but will also commonly provide free professional photography and floorplans for listings.

It is rare but a couple of agencies allow the agents to keep nearly all of the commission but charge larger fees, sometimes monthly, like renting a chair at a salon.

Agencies in nyc typically do NOT provide leads to their agents, except for very rarely, in store front locations they will offer the opportunity to 'work the desk' in which case in exchange for greeting visitors, you are welcome to try to convince them to work with you personally. Alternatively, if inquiries come into your agency manager or to the front desk they are doled out to someone, but it is usually not you (;-)). They are spread around among all agents, which is typically a lot of agents, or they are funneled directly to the people who are making the most money. Yes, in real estate, the people who make the most money are treated much better overall. Sales has always been like that. It is what it is.

Leads come from a few places… if you have been doing this for a while they can come from referrals – in my experience, those tend to be the best leads. These prospects trust you a little already and sought you out preferentially. Alternatively, if you have a listing (an apartment to sell) you will get to meet the buyers who come to it, and you are welcome to try to convert them to buyer-customers if they are not interested in the place you are selling. This is always, though, a slightly awkward relationship at first because, of course, you are supposed to be acting as if the place you are trying to sell is the only place worth buying on the planet earth and so moving to "Hey so not feeling this place? – yeah – no problem – let's talk about other places you might like more that I can help you find" may have to wait. A common strategy is to take these buyers information and wait a few days until you are certain they have zero interest in the place you are selling if you can- and then offer to send them other listings.

Alternatively agents will make cold calls to sellers who's exclusive contracts have expired to see if they might want to list with them, or, they can also search for sellers who are selling their own place (FSBOs – which agents refer to, awkwardly, as 'fizz-bos') but these are very hard to convert because selling your own place is frankly such a terrible idea in NYC (my feelings are described in the next chapter) that the people who are doing it tend to be rather die-hard about it – with some personal or philosophical chip on their shoulder that compels them.

# SHOULD YOU USE AN AGENT?

**For Sellers:**

Time is money in real estate and to that end I'll make the first answer easy and short. Should you use an agent to sell your property even if you are prepared to sell it yourself? **Yes** you absolutely should. Do NOT sell it yourself unless you already have a pre-screened buyer and even then for the love of God, please make sure your real estate attorney is really good.

Why is this such an obvious answer for me? Several reasons. Selling places in NYC is challenging even for people who have done it before. Listing your property is going to cost you money anyway and getting maximum exposure for your place that it is visible to buyer's agents is going to be hard without going through the kind of listing system used by an agency that disseminates to all other agencies, sometimes known as an MLS, or Multiple Listing Service.

Also, buyers' agents are unlikely to send their customers to you unless they are going to be getting paid their typical half of the commission which means that you will have to either sacrifice prospective customers loyal to their buyer's agents or pay half of the commission to them. Plus, in my experience, even having the owner *present* when you show a listing is a turn off to customers as they try to imagine the place as their own. It's very difficult to sound credible extolling the virtues of your own apartment, plus owners tend to lack the objectivity to prioritize the messaging that appeals most to current buyers. I like to DIY almost everything, but after a bunch of years in the industry, just please trust me, even if maximizing your profit is your goal your time means nothing to you, and you are in no hurry to sell, this is a job you want to outsource.

**For Buyers:**

As to whether to use a buyer's agent in a purchase, while in most cases it makes sense to use one, there is more room for discussion here. Sometimes, but very rarely, a particularly difficult seller's agent, generally only ones at tiny mom and pop agencies, with lower priced listings, in boroughs outside of Manhattan-- will make a purchase more challenging for a customer with a buyer's agent by prioritizing customers that are acting solo because they do not want to share the commission. Even in these situations, I would argue that a seasoned agent will know the signs of a selling agent that is avoiding co-broking, and can either remedy that with persistence, or, if they are especially honest – will offer to give you up as a customer and send you directly to the listing without them.

It's my belief that the upside of using a buyer's agent far outweighs whatever deficit in the rare event that the selling agent wants to avoid them. In many cases, the selling agent is even *happy* to share commission, because it means they won't have to manage both parts of the transaction... reducing their workload so they can focus on other properties.

The most important advantage though of using an agent for a purchase is the agent's familiarity with the weird NYC process. With experience they know what to look for in a particular sale in order to give the buyer protection from unscrupulous sellers, helping to highlight properties that might be especially desirable, and steering them away from properties that look great on the outside but are actually duds.

In addition, real estate agents work on sourcing properties full time so while you are working doing whatever you do that allows you to purchase NYC real estate -- they can be researching comps and scrutinizing listings. Once you are in contract, they can solve problems and answer questions that might arise, protect you from the selling agent, and represent your interests against the seller. They can also create an appealing board package (or condo application) on your behalf, while working with your attorney, who may not have much time for you, and your bank, who might sometimes assign you someone more junior who occasionally needs some help.

All in all, from what I have seen, people purchasing above or below $500K in Manhattan, ALWAYS benefit from having a buyer's agent, and people purchasing under that, in other boroughs, generally do too if the person they are working with is willing to be honest about the potential for running into the rare selling agent that *really* doesn't want to co-broke and there is a plan in place on how to handle that.

# HOW TO PICK A REAL ESTATE AGENT AND MAXIMIZE YOUR RELATIONSHIP WITH THEM

There are a ridiculous number of real estate agents in NYC, and if we are going to be honest about it, the barrier to entry into this profession is very low given the cost of the thing being sold. In fact, it is shocking to me how low it is. It is my impression that it is infinitely more difficult to get hired to sell Louis Vuitton bags which max out around 35K than it is to become a real estate agent. It is no wonder that real estate sales is not considered the most loveable or trustworthy profession. There is no worse feeling than realizing halfway through a transaction that involves all of the money that you may have saved for many years that your agent sucks.

So, what do you do? Let's break it down. Here are two things you are probably worried about and want to avoid in an agent. 1. Someone who doesn't know what they are doing 2. Someone who is going to lie to you about everything. The first one is easier to identify than the second of course. Kind of.

There is a way I recommend you can screen for the first concern, and I feel guilty saying it, because it unfairly eliminates a whole category of real estate agents who might be amazing, that would also probably have a higher level of enthusiasm and might need the work most. Pick an agent who has been working actively in NYC real estate for over 5 years. Ideally from a major agency. Ok, maybe three years if they seem really great.

Why? Not because they will have necessarily become better at the job during that time, though they might have learned some things-- but because the industry is very competitive, so unless their real estate career is being propped up by a rich romantic partner (some percentage), a trust fund, or a robust side hustle, if they have managed to pay their bills for five years on NYC real estate sales alone, it is probably some indication that they are not terrible at the job. You can only massively screw up so many deals before people start to find out and you don't get hired anymore, so longevity-- if you are in fact making enough money to survive-- is significant.

After you have selected an agent:

Once you have identified an agent you like and think can do the job- feel free to confirm a few things about their business practice, aka . trustworthiness. Will they like that you are asking these questions? No, they will not. No one enjoys having their professional approach questioned, especially by someone mostly unfamiliar with what they do – but feel free to do it anyway, albeit politely. Blame me and this guide if you want.

1. If they are selling for you – confirm that they will treat all buyer interest the same – both with and without buyer's agents. No returning direct deal customers calls first. Your best buyer might be the one with the agent.

2. If they are acting as your buying agent... ask them to let you know if they sense that the selling agent is being difficult about sharing the commission

Despite the things I recommend that you look out for in selecting someone to help you purchase or sell your most expensive asset... there are some things you might want to be generous about that will also help your transaction.

1. Offer your selling agent exclusivity. When you hire an agent to list your property – it is typical to sign an exclusive agreement with that person. I have had sellers occasionally ask why it is to their advantage to limit themselves to only one person or agency to sell their property. The honest answer is twofold. One, no one is going to try as hard, or care as much, about selling your place if they think they might do the job only to discover that some other agent is going into contract on it. Also – nearly no agent will offer premium resources like professional floorplans or photography on a place that is not theirs exclusively. Most agencies won't reimburse those expenses without an exclusive contract.

2. Offer your buying agent exclusivity. I'd say 95 percent of my customers choose to only work with me and no one else when buying even though there is no signed agreement. They do this knowing that I will exercise my full personal and professional resources

to help them find the place they want. I recommend that you, similarly, offer loyalty to your buyer's agent throughout the time you choose to work with them, for several entirely self-serving reasons.

The primary one is that the best, smartest, hardest working, buyer's agents, HATE knowing they are in competition with other agents for obvious reasons. In fact, the authentically best, agents I know – the ones with the resources and intelligence to discover good deals, unique spaces, and solve potential problems for you…just won't work with you if you are not willing to offer loyalty once the process starts.

Or at least, unofficially, they won't. Sure, an agent might tolerate a customer that they suspect is working with other people, but their effort is always going to be limited, and that is not what you want. You can search listings yourself but the skills a good agent has that you really need, that can help your purchase in a material way, are significant, and agents who understand the value they add will feel at best annoyed by a lack of loyalty, at worst, will just not try and will just string you along.

3. Plan to pay a 6% commission if you are a seller – maybe negotiable down to 5.5% or 5% if the agent's manager will allow it – depending on the details of your sale (though if they say they can't lower it – that might be true). I know of literally no agents-- in all the years I have been doing this, that will charge you less than 5%, ever, that you want to have represent you. None.

Why not? Commissions below 5% are generally only considered by smaller agencies which are too small to offer a marketing presence that will benefit your property most. Alternatively – it may indicate that the only way an agent can get listings is to offer themselves at what is considered industry-wide - a discounted price. Also, a lower commission makes any buyers agent's split less attractive too. Buyer's agents probably won't consciously hide your listing from their customers (though they might) – but they certainly could be less enthusiastic about getting their buyers interest in it. Please just trust me on this. Just pay the commission for the agent you think is best -- it really is likely to end up economically even in the end, or better, for you in terms of the speed of your sale and increased closing price.

# REAL ESTATE ATTORNEYS: YES, YOU SHOULD HAVE ONE-WHAT THEY DO FOR YOU AND HOW TO PICK ONE

In NYC real estate agents don't do as much after contract signing as agents do in other places. Ok - that's not entirely true- there are always plenty of complicated issues in an NYC transaction that a pro-active and experienced real estate agent can help smooth out after a contract is signed. But relative to other states, where agents are allowed to write contracts themselves, amend other legal documents, and create legally binding agreements- agents in NYC do not do these things. It is so overwhelmingly expected that both the buyer and seller in a NYC purchase will have legal representation that I really can't even imagine how the process might work without both a buying and selling attorney. In over a decade I have never seen either party choose to be unrepresented. Why would you?

The attorney's role begins once you have agreed on a price and terms. As soon as a sale price is negotiated, and any contingencies are determined, (the most common ones being whether or not approval for a mortgage will be a requirement of the purchase ((*a mortgage contingency*)) or if an inspection will be a requirement (much less common--*an inspection contingency*) the seller's real estate agent will create what is known as a *'deal sheet'* (a form with information relevant to the creation of the contract.) including all the terms and contact info for the buyer, seller, and their agents. This is sent out immediately to both attorneys and is the basis for the contract. For this reason, it is essential that you have an attorney selected before you submit an offer because you will need them to receive the deal sheet right away.

If you are the buyer - after the contract is sent out your attorney will begin the process of reviewing the pros and cons of your purchase in a process known as *'due diligence'* They will ask to see a copy of something called an offering plan which will be provided by the listing agent, or if it is new construction-a prospectus... These are large documents full of details about the building. They will also ask for the building's financials and will often read the buildings minutes --. a weird little bit of protocol, in case you are interested, is that some buildings won't release the minutes to the attorney-- and so it may be that your attorney, or someone from their office, will have to go physically to the building in person in order to read them.

Like with any profession - not all attorneys are great. Some are, but the range is vast – from 'problem-solving-protect-you-from-everything genius' attorneys to people it's hard to believe passed the bar. Do not presume that an Esq. after someone's name means they know what to do. So how do you vet this person? Positive reviews are unreliable – they can be written by friends and relatives. Negative reviews are somewhat more reliable - but of course unhappy people tend to write more reviews.

In terms of what to look for in an attorney - a few things come to mind:

1. Attorneys charge a flat fee – Do NOT be cheap with your attorney. Like with many things – if an attorney's rate is especially low – it is likely because they are not good enough to charge more. Pick one in the middle or the top.
2. Attorneys - even good ones – can be kind of stingy with their time… the flat fee system means that relative to other kinds of legal professionals they have to work with volume and are often overwhelmed with customers. If you are new to the process of buying or selling you might want to let your prospective attorney know that and see how they respond – if they assure you that they will make time for you – that is a good sign.
3. Please use a New York City based attorney… and ideally a real estate specific one – I have seen transactions get unnecessarily derailed because one attorney was based in even nearby places like Long Island, and despite insisting that they understood the process of closing a NYC co-op, it became quickly clear they did not. You want someone who has closed many of the exact kind of property you are selling or buying-feel free to ask. In the case of the Long Island attorney-- the customer ultimately had to switch mid-way– something you do not want to have to do.
4. Sometimes you might want to use a friend or relative attorney and you would think this would be a great idea – and maybe sometimes it is. But not for nothin' I have seen this get f****d up more than once – though I understand sometimes you must do it. In this case

just please make additionally sure that your real estate agent is good so that there is someone for them to collaborate with in case your friend turns out not to be as good as you had hoped— having them work with your agent could save the deal and maybe your friendship.
5. In the end, like with your real estate agent, and also your mortgage broker – just please make sure that they have done several transactions – ideally recently – very similar to the one you are trying to complete.

# WHAT'S IN A REAL ESTATE CONTRACT? : WHAT AM I AGREEING TO?

Consideration of the details of a sales contract is, perhaps surprisingly, the least time-consuming part of most transactions - at least from the buyer or seller's point of view, unless you are trading ('trading' is the cool kid's insider-y term meaning 'selling or buying') something with a lot of unusual traits. Why? Because it is, for the most part, standard to most nyc real estate transactions and based on a template.

Nearly all typical sales use roughly the same base contract and then amend that. It's not carefully considered and crafted -- it's more like the lease you sign for a rental except with a lot more money at stake. Some paragraphs might be 'redacted' (crossed out) and then there might be 'riders' or 'addendums' at the end that are additions that are for the purpose of clarifying unique details of the sale or sometimes attorneys like to be extra diligent by adding some protections for either their buyers or sellers that are not part of the standard contract format.

The contract first makes its appearance after an offered price and purchasing terms are negotiated and accepted. After that, the selling agent sends out something called a 'deal sheet' which is an email shared with both attorneys, with all contact information for buyers, sellers, and their representatives. The 'deal sheet' includes the details of the deal, asking price, accepted price etc. etc. After this is received by both attorneys... the selling attorney creates and sends the contract to the buyer's agent for signing.

This contract will include the agreed upon terms of the deal, which may include:

1. The agreed price
2. Whether or not the buyer is financing and the percentage the buyer will be putting down
3. Any contingencies. Most common are a *financing contingency* (the buyer is released from the contract in the event they cannot procure financing) or an *inspection contingency* (the buyer is entitled to review an inspection report and get access to the unit and building in order to do an independent inspection, before signing).
4. The length of time allowed before the buyer's commitment letter from the bank is due (this shows the finalization of their loan and is a major milestone towards closing)
5. The date the board package or condo application is due
6. An estimated closing date – which is often considered flexible within a 30 day range
7. Any special conditions of the sale, such as whether the seller might want to rent-back the unit for a period of time after the sale is finalized (not a popular option and a turn off to some buyers-- but sometimes necessary)
8. A list of items that are included or excluded from the sale... for instance, light fixtures; typically presumed to be included but if the seller wishes

to keep them, they would be listed in the 'exclusions' section of the contract.

**For Buyers:** Once your attorney receives the contract, they will review it and will *not* automatically share it with you or your agent. In fact unless you specifically ask to see it, it is more common, *not* to send you, nor your agent, until they have reviewed it, and in some cases – you will not see it until they are ready for you to sign it.

Why? Essentially, the honest answer is; if you trust your attorney, you don't need it. The contract is dense and potentially confusing and might stress you out unnecessarily. I know this may sound condescending – you're a smart person capable of understanding a contract - but the phrasing of some parts of a standard sales contract are honestly kind of weird and its interpretation is based in precedent which you couldn't possibly know – but your attorney, hopefully, does. In fact, that's kind of their job, to interpret and modify the contract so that it is most advantageous for you. Also, the time involved in explaining the contract to you is not built into your fee at all and, honestly, for real estate attorneys who work on volume with a flat fee generally it would be nearly career destroying to do describe the details of every contract with every customer.

Having said this though--it is 100 percent your right to ask your attorney for a copy of your contract as soon as they receive it -- and even to pester them for answers to any concerns you have – but just please be fair – remember their time is *literally* worth money to them so maybe send email instead of calling and be ready to wait for an answer. If you have hired an attorney, you trust it's unlikely that they are encouraging you to sign a contract that is selling you out somehow—so try not to freak out even if something seems wrong though at the same time it is your right to feel informed to your satisfaction before signing.

**For Sellers:** Once the buyer's attorney receives the contract, they will need your agent to provide a copy of the offering plan, and building financials, and will begin a process of reviewing the contract and details of the building. This process is known as 'due diligence' which can take anywhere from several days to a couple of weeks. You are welcome to try to put a limit on the amount of time allowed to do this, but they might resist, and it is not common. The presumption is that they buyer is as motivated to sign quickly as much as you are eager to have them do it, because, without signatures by both parties ( a 'fully executed' contract), there is no legal commitment between you, so there is a risk they might lose the property as much as you risk losing them as a buyer.

During this time the buyer's attorney may attempt to negotiate details of the contract, review the financials of the building, try to discover any repair history, and possibly read board minutes, in order to understand the pros and cons of the purchase better for their client. There will likely be some back and forth between your attorney and the buyer's attorney.

Once the buyer's attorney has reviewed everything, and any agreed upon amendments to the contract have been made, if they and their client feel that the purchase makes sense, they will invite the buyers to sign the contract and leave a 10% deposit in their escrow account to bind it. The amount collected there will be 10% even if the buyers intend to put down 20% or more in the purchase ultimately as a down payment. In standard contracts – this 10% is the amount that will be given to you, the seller, if the buyer chooses to pull out of the deal ---unless there are terms described that might mitigate that.

These mitigating caveats are called 'contingencies.' The most common one would be a *mortgage contingency* suggesting that if the buyer has made every reasonable effort to obtain a loan and is unable to get one-- they would be allowed to withdraw their offer without losing their deposit. Some offers, even one's with financing, are made *without* a mortgage contingency which makes them, of course, more attractive. A financed purchase without a mortgage contingency means that, if the buyer were not to successfully procure financing, they would be compelled to complete the purchase in cash or lose the deposit.

Once, ultimately, the contract is signed by the buyers and 10% is collected into their attorneys account, the contract is returned to the seller for signing. Not until the seller has signed the contract and shared a copy of the signed document back to the buyers' attorney is the contract considered 'fully executed' and the sale is secured. Any time up until that moment either party may withdraw without consequences. For this reason, there is a fair bit of nervousness on both sides before the process is complete.

# YOUR CLOSING – WHAT TO BRING – WHAT TO EXPECT

No matter what kind of property you are buying or selling, closings are more similar than different. Makes sense --while your closing is a big deal for you - all the other parties involved have presumably done many before. Despite the immense number of documents exchanged (yes – *tons* of paper documents – the real estate closing process is still typically very paper heavy, almost nothing is done online ) with a roomful of people who know what they are doing the process is surprisingly streamlined. In fact, I am often surprised by how often the players at the closing table will recognize each other from previous closings. Out of hundreds of banks that provide mortgages, thousands of attorneys who practice real estate law, and the large number of management companies that handle buildings in NYC, city real estate is not a big world.

This is not to say that closings aren't complicated events...the number of details is mind boggling. In fact, that would be my first piece of advice to you – do not panic (presuming you trust your attorney ((please God tell me that by now I have convinced you to hire an attorney that you trust.)) if you do not understand every detail of your own closing. Sure, there is nothing going on at that table that you couldn't understand if someone were to slow the process down and explain it to you – but no one is going to do that. Once the closing gets underway – everyone there has a job to do that requires a lot of focus on details and the whole thing goes very fast. In fact, to some degree – that is the goal – to get through the closing as quickly as possible.

Generally, your attorney will make some basic effort to describe each of the many documents you personally will be signing – but even that explanation will typically be very brief and so even with the papers that require your agreement, no one will explain anything else going on there. The table is buzzy and papers will be traded back and forth between the parties present.

There are generally two distinct kinds of activities happening at the closing simultaneously: closing the sale of the property, and closing the loan on the property (the 'pay off') if the seller had one, and getting confirmation of the new loan if the buyer is getting one. In the end, - you will receive keys (be sure you recieve a mailbox key, a storage unit key, and a front door key if there are these) and a deed or a proprietary lease (hold on to this document. The piece of paper itself is very important.)

Just for your reference…here are the documents you will be signing at the closing:

**For Buyers:**

The Truth in Lending Statement defines the details of any mortgage loan.

The mortgage and the note, these are two distinct documents, one explains the details of the mortgage itself and the other defines repayment terms.

Property Deed; transfers the ownership to you.

A variety of affidavits. These documents confirm various

statements made by either party. For example, sellers frequently sign an affidavit stating they have not incurred any property liens.

The Real Estate Settlement Procedures Act (RESPA) statement defines all closing costs, also called the HUD-1 closing statement. You will want to have this document for income tax purposes and if you sell.

Any home insurance policies proving coverage.

In case you are curious about who all those people gathered around your closing table are---they are

1. A representative for the buyer's bank if they are getting financing (your banker themselves will not attend)
2. If there is still outstanding financing on the place – a representative from the seller's bank will be present to accept what is known as the 'payoff' (the transfer of funds to pay off the seller's loan on the property)
3. The buyer's attorney
4. The seller's attorney
5. A representative of the building's management company if you are purchasing a co-op or condo
6. Sometimes the buyer and seller (though not always— the attorney can be given proxy)
7. Sometimes the selling or buying agent or both (It can occasionally be helpful to have them there to clarify details or discuss possible fixes that need to be negotiated from the walk through – though often they have no actual role there and just come for moral support and to pick up their commission check at the end. Agents are pretty superfluous to the closing and it's not unheard of for them not to even sit at the closing table or to be looking at their phone the entire time – feel free to ask them to get you coffee or water

if you want. Brokers don't hate me.)

# CLOSING COSTS

*Buyers:*

**Condo:**

Own Attorney: $2,000+ up

Managing Agent Application Fee: $300 +

Credit Report Fee: $75 - $100 per applicant

Lead-Based Paint Disclosure Fee: $0 - $50

Mansion Tax: Purchase Price Mansion Tax

    Less than $999,999 - 0.00%

    $1,000,000 – $1,999,999 - 1.00%

    $2,000,000 – $2,999,999 - 1.25%

    $3,000,000 – $4,999,999 - 1.50%

    $5,000,000 – $9,999,999 - 2.25%

    $10,000,000 – $14,999,999 - 3.25%

    $15,000,000 – $19,999,999 - 3.50%

    $20,000,000 – $24,999,999 - 3.75%

    $25,000,000 or more - 3.90%

Move-in Deposit: $500 - $1,000 (refundable if no damage)

Common charges, real estate taxes, and insurance: prorated as of the closing

Condo Mortgage Associated Fees: prorated as of the closing

Mortgage Tax: (Paid by the buyer, condominium/townhouses

only, when financing

Recording Tax Sales under $500,000: 1.8% of the entire mortgage

Recording Tax Sales over $500,000: 1.925% of the entire mortgage

Application, Credit Check, etc.: $500+ up

Appraisal: $250+ up

Bank Attorney: $500+ up

UCC-1 Filing: $50+ up

Recognition Agreement Fee: $200 + up

Lien Search: $350

Fee Title Insurance: Approx $450 per $100,000

Mortgage Title Insurance: Approx. $200 per $100,000

Recording Fees: $200 - $300

Origination Costs - Points: 0-3% of the loan value

Departmental Searches: $200 - $400

Real Estate Tax Escrow: 2-6 months

**If Purchased Directly from Sponsor *New Developments:**

NYC and NYS Property Transfer Tax

Property Sale Price /NY State Transfer tax /NYC Transfer Tax Total Transfer Tax

$499,999 and less - 0.40% 1.00% 1.40%

$500,000 - $1,999,999 - 0.40% 1.425% 1.825%
$2,000,000 - $2,999,999 - 0.40% 1.425% 1.825%
$3,000,000 - $4,999,999 - 0.65% 1.425% 2.075%
$5,000,000 - $9,999,999 - 0.65% 1.425% 2.075%
$10,000,000 - $14,999,999 - 0.65% 1.425% 2.075%
$15,000,000 - $19,999,999 - 0.65% 1.425% 2.075%
$20,000,000 - $24,999,999 - 0.65% 1.425% 2.075%
$25,000,000 or more - 0.65% 1.425% 2.075%

Sponsor's Attorney Fee: $1,500

**Co-op:**

Own Attorney: $2,000 + up

Bank Fees: Points: 0% to 3% of loan value

Application, credit check, etc: $500+

Bank Attorney: $700+

Miscellaneous Bank Fees: $500+

Lien Search: $300

UCC-1 Filing: $100

Move-in deposit: $500+

Recognition Agreement Fee: $200

Maintenance Adjustment: Pro-rated for the months of closing.

Mansion Tax: 1%+ of purchase price for any purchase over 1m

**Townhouse:**

Own Attorney: $1,500 +

Engineer/Inspection Report: $750 - $2000

Termite Inspection: $200 - $500

Mansion Tax: 1%+ of entire purchase price over 1m

Townhouse Mortgage Associated Origination costs- points: 0 - 3% of loan value

UCC-1 Filing: $50 +

Appraisal Fee: $300 +

Application Fee (Credit Report/Appraisal): $500 +

Recording Tax Sales under $500,000: 1.75% of entire mortgage

Recording Tax Sales over $500,000: 1.875% of entire mortgage

Title Insurance, Title Search & Recording Fees: up to 0.5% of purchase

Building Searches: $200 - $400

Recording Charge: $17 per document plus $5 per page

NYS Transfer Tax: $4 per $1,000 of the purchase price

## *Sellers:*

**Condo / Townhouse:**

Broker(s): Typically 5%-6%

Seller's attorney (negotiated flat rate): $2,500±

NY City Transfer Tax: 1% of sales price for sales of $500,000; or less 1.425% for sales in excess of $500K

NY State Transfer Tax: $2 per $500 (or 0.4% of sales price)

Miscellaneous title company fees (if seller has mortgage): $450±

Move-out deposit or fees (condo): $1,000 (varies)

Managing agent fees (condo): $500±

**Co-op:**

Broker(s): Typically 5% - 6%

Seller's attorney (negotiated flat rate): $2,500±

NY City Transfer Tax: 1% of sales price for sales of $500,000; or less 1.425% for sales in excess of $500K

NY State Transfer Tax: $2 per $500 (or 0.4% of sales price)

Flip tax (if any)*: Often 2-3%, consult managing agent

Managing agent fee: $600±

Stock Transfer Tax: $0.05 per share

Move-out deposit or fees: $1,000 (varies)

Payoff bank attorney (if seller has mortgage): $500±

UCC-3 filing (if seller has mortgage): Up to $100 per loan

*Flip taxes vary on amount and by whom they are payable (buyer or seller)

# THE APPRAISAL – WHAT IS THE PROCESS AND WHAT IF, GOD FORBID, IT COMES IN LOW?

When things go right the appraisal on a NYC apartment goes mostly unnoticed. Your offer is accepted, and then a couple of weeks later, as you are busy supplying paperwork to the bank and organizing an application-- often unbeknownst to you, the selling agent meets up with an independent appraiser (not uncommonly a 20 year old from Long Island unfamiliar with the area) to value the place you are in contract on. They use local comparative units as a guide.

Occasionally the agent will proactively provide the appraiser with comps, (which they should probably, ethically, ignore so they are not being led by someone with stake in the transaction- but whatever. New York City.) and within a week or so your bank is told the appraisal has come in, shockingly, at exactly the number of your accepted offer. Does this seem like an unlikely coincidence? Of course, it is… it's nonsense, but that's how it works. Appraisers are not in the business of making people's lives miserable or ruining deals – nor are they typically super geniuses at valuating property in fact in a place where prices change so briskly like nyc it would be fair to suggest that, really, property is worth, essentially, the highest price offered for it.

The only time you ever really think about the appraisal at all is in the unlikely event that it comes in low and then there can be some excitement, as you, seller or buyer, try to figure out what to do...but don't worry, there are a few possibilities outside of just walking away. Mostly, I have only seen appraisals come in low a handful of times in over a decade of doing this and in both cases they were in areas where the sales prices had risen so fast the comps in the area had not caught up.

However, in the unlikely event your appraisal is lower than your price, there are several standard options in terms of how to handle this 1. The seller can choose to reduce the selling price to whatever number the appraisal came in 2. The buyer can accept a smaller loan and put down more in cash to make up the difference. Remember, bank appraisals are in no way an absolute determinant of the actual value of an apartment– it is just a measure used by the bank to determine how much they want to lend, so choosing to make up the difference is not always a terrible idea. 3. The seller and buyer can split the difference (duh.) 4. You can request a reappraisal if you disagree with the number. There is generally a charge to do this -- but if you feel that the appraiser might have missed some significant comps that would justify the higher price – it might be worthwhile.

# FOR SELLERS: WHAT'S IN AN EXCLUSIVE CONTRACT WITH A REAL ESTATE AGENCY?

The process of picking the right agent for your sale is not an easy one. The job of a real estate salesperson in NYC can be sometimes really easy (sorry NYC real estate agents- I imagine that statement will be as popular as saying that being a stay-at-home-parent is easy) but, just as often, it can be *tremendously* challenging and complex and an utter pain in the ass. If, as a seller, you want the best outcome you will want someone good and it *will* make a difference.

Sure, anyone can show up dressed nicely, open the door to your place, and show it to people. If you have plenty of buyer interest from perfect buyers who make lots of high offers and follow through with their side of the purchase like clockwork, then, of course, any person who can use email, and won't lose your keys, will do. However, things rarely go that way and even under the best of circumstances, an agent who is better at sales or can compose a compelling listing, manage appointments properly, sell your place well, and negotiate offers, will still get higher numbers. There is an art to inspiring higher prices for properties that involves sales skills and making sure that the details buyers want to hear are shared in an appealing way. Not everyone can do this.

All agents will ask you to sign what is known as an *exclusive listing agreement (or contract)* and it will include these important details:

1. The beginning and end dates that the individual or team you select has the exclusive right to sell your place. During this time no one else can sell it, and *you* can't sell it, without owing the agent commission. A duration of six months is typical.
2. The listing price for your property
3. The amount of commission that will be paid to the agent once they have procured a buyer for the sale at the price you have specified in the contract – 6% is typical though can, occasionally, be negotiated.
4. A separate disclosure sheet from the State Dept, filled out by your agent and signed by you, confirming that you understand two things.
    a. Your agent, *legally*, works *only* for you – often in competition with the buying party's interests. Presumably this means that you, the seller, want *more* money and the buyer wants to pay *less* money. Your agent is supposed to do whatever is legally available to get you top dollar for your property - they are *not* being paid to work out a fair deal.
    b. *If* either the buyer doesn't have their own buying agent, *or* they do have a buying agent who happens to work for the same agency as your selling agent, your agent is *still* obliged to work exclusively for you even though straddling both sides of the transaction while remaining faithful to you is hard. The buying party will receive a similar disclosure form reminding them that. In a 'dual-

agency' situation (where the buyer has no agent) I like to teasingly remind the buyer all the time throughout the transaction that I am not working in their best interests because I work for the seller... this seems to both build trust with the buyer, leading them to feel that I will honestly disclose other things that might not be favorable to them —putting them at ease, plus it reminds them that I really am there to get the most money for the seller and perform my fiduciary duty.

5. A Housing and Anti-Discrimination form - This form offers a reminder that if you feel that you have been subject to discrimination during the sales process by any party involved -- you are welcome to report it to The Division of Human Rights Complaints Dept. and provides contact info therein.

A question that sometimes comes up about having an exclusive relationship with an agent or team is why you should have one at all. After all, wouldn't it be better to have multiple agents and agencies competing to sell your property? In theory it would be --but in reality – you might be scraping the bottom of the NYC real estate agent barrel in order to accomplish that. Sure, there are agents and agencies that are willing to work on what is known as an 'open listing' (one without any exclusive affiliation) but, between you and me, they aren't generally very good.

Most good agents won't do it for fear of wasting a bunch of time trying to sell a place only to discover their competition has beaten them to it – but also plenty of better agencies discourage it. Without an exclusive agreement – the agency won't list it – even internally. Personally, I wouldn't work on something (not in residential real estate anyway, in commercial it is more common) without an agreement-- unless the commission offered was so incredibly high that the risk of maybe wasting a bunch of time was totally overwhelmed by the huge prospective reward and even then, I'd want to know I was in a very small pool. Also, listing a place to best effect involves a solid presence online and duplicate listings on real estate platforms aren't allowed, plus few agents would want to pay for professional photos, staging, floorplan, or spend the time writing good copy, unless they knew they would be free to market, show, and sell the place without interference.

# FOR SELLERS: HOW TO PRICE YOUR PROPERTY?

Determining an appropriate starting number for your place right out of the gate and knowing what your pricing/negotiation strategy is going to be (including the lowest number you will accept ) is an important decision. If you are talking to several real estate agents about what your property might sell for as you decide who to sign an exclusive agreement with --please know that it is not uncommon for the highest numbers, you hear to be inflated-- contrived to win your signature on that agent's exclusive agreement.

I hate sharing this fact—real estate agents have an incredibly bad rap overall in terms of trustworthiness, and people tend to think they are lying about *everything*—even when they are not—but inflating sales prices to get a listing is, unfortunately, very very common. Many brokers will just tell you what you want to hear – or just agree to the number you suggest, even if they suspect it is way too high. This practice is both unhelpful, misleading, and also can put more trustworthy, and arguably better, brokers are at a disadvantage.

So how do you figure out what price is right for your place? First, unless you know that your broker is both talented at pricing and trustworthy, personally, I would attempt to verify any numbers they give you by asking them to share the comps they used to arrive at those prices. Even then, you might also want to look for recently sold properties with similar features in your immediate area on StreetEasy. Remember to focus mainly on properties that have already sold as opposed to being currently on the market – because then you will know that those are post-negotiation, or, actual, prices someone wanted to pay and not potentially inflated attempts.

To make matters worse there is a common misperception that agents will suggest pricing that is too *low* for your property in order to achieve a speedy sale. This is only ever true *after* you have signed an exclusive agreement. And just in case you are a pie in the sky optimist and think you have found the one broker who really understands the true value of your place, I have never *ever* been surprised by the final sale price of a home.

I'm not a skeptic. I like slightly aspirational pricing, in fact it's my favorite strategy, but there is an upper limit to every place that 'positive thinking' or 'putting it out there' does not change. In fact I have seen better agents – the ones you want to be working with (who actually get the highest numbers for sales) go as far as to walk away from listings if sellers refuse to price within the realm of reality. Bless their hearts, they don't want to lie to the seller and they don't want to waste anyone's time.

Once you have some confidence in what your place is realistically worth on the current market there are several possible strategies for how to sell it.

The first is the most obvious: price it exactly the way you think is right and plan not to reduce your price very much (unless you *have* to sell, in which case-- do what you need to do, just make sure the buyer doesn't find out about your eagerness).

The second pricing possibility (and this is my favorite): is to list it for roughly 10% above what you think is the "right" number. It leaves room for negotiation and It allows for an error in pricing in case it turns out buyers surprise you by wanting to pay more than anticipated. Also, this strategy might help because, of course, some of pricing is perception – so a higher starting price (even if it is eventually reduced) might encourage people to value the place more highly in their minds.

If though, using this strategy, you *do* discover that you want to reduce your price based on customer feedback (either visitors universally commenting on the price, or discovering there is very low attendance at open houses, and fewer than average requests for showings) I advise not to wait more than a few weeks to reduce it. Make that correction sooner than later so that it still appears to be *relatively* new online at the new, lower, price.

The third strategy: which you tend to see more in a seller's market, is to price low. Why? To inspire more visitors to come see the property--excited by what a deal it appears to be with the intention of encouraging bidding upwards. Especially with most buyers using an online search to find places to buy, with high and low purchase prices included in their parameters, choosing a lower listing price directly equals appearing in more prospective customers search results. A low pricing strategy might also make sense if you need to sell very fast and would consider letting it go for the lower number even if that is not your preference. You then can hope that having lots of showings and bustling open houses might spur the ever-famous 'bidding war' with buyers pushing up the price through a sense of competition.

Once an exclusive contract is signed – something to be aware of is that, technically, if the agent is able to procure any buyer meeting the number on the contract—the seller is contractually obliged to pay them commission. So, if you decide to go with a low pricing strategy, with the intention of raising it, just know that you will owe the agent commission if they arrive at the number you have agreed on. In practice, I have never actually seen an agent insist that their job is done once they reach that price if you have agreed beforehand that it is part of a plan to increase the price through competition- but in theory it could happen.

Ultimately the market decides what the right price is going to be, and in NYC that can change very quickly, from month to month even, based on factors totally outside of you and your agent's control - but knowing what range you feel confident about with some upfront agreement on strategy, can certainly make the process smoother.

# FOR SELLERS: BEFORE YOU SELL –
## Renovation and Repairs

Every seller wants to do what they can to maximize the profit from their sale, and in some cases, if they can afford to pretty up the place some, it can make the buyers first impression better and potentially lead to higher offers. However, there are also plenty of times when I have counselled sellers not to bother making changes beyond painting because I didn't believe the fix would equal the money spent on it.

So here are some things that come up as you consider renovating to sell ---and my thoughts on them.

1. Was there a previous leak that was your or the building's responsibility that has been rectified? Of course you should disclose it --but that doesn't mean you have to *show* it to prospective buyers once it's corrected. The best way to impress buyers is by pointing at a completely flat, dry, surface and telling the story of how quickly, effectively, and permanently the leak was repaired.

2. People will, of course, pay more for renovated kitchens and bathrooms, sure, but will they pay as much as your renovation will cost? And will the renovation you do meet the standards of your new

buyers? In general, unless there are glaring issues with your existing kitchen and bathroom (leaking toilet, massively stained countertop, etc.), in 2023 2024 NYC, I'd say leave it alone, and presume your buyers will renovate. Or, if you do have some kind of glaring issue, missing backsplash tiles, missing drawer fronts, etc.... yes, replace those things... In general, My general rule for fixes before a sale is that if it is something that looks outstandingly wrong such that it draws attention to itself – fix it. If not – leave it alone. There are some exceptions to this though –

    a. Complete gut reno: If you can gut a shabbier apartment and cheaply make everything pristine—especially in smaller apartments – it can sometimes make sense. If it makes a formerly very dated place move-in ready for individuals or smaller groups – sometimes you can make money. Look at comps and do the math. I have seen this work.

    b. Paint. You do want to paint. You also want to patch any cracks or holes in any room where that is called for. Nothing says 'dilapidated' like cracks in a wall or ceiling. If you can't afford to paint more than one room go for the entry and the living room. Added bonus if you paint the interior (yes that's right) of a coat closet, or the closet in the bedroom. Why? Because it's cheap and easy and since most people don't --- it will have a positive impact because it will be a surprise. Bonus points if you have your broker leave the closet door closed or just slightly ajar with the light on inside so when people open it they are dazzled by how bright it is. And yes, everything must be shades of cream or white. Don't be fancy. You want mass appeal and the effect of more light not cool personal style.

c. Adding bedrooms. Are there other units like yours in your building that have been converted into more legal bedrooms? Can you convert legally into more bedrooms? The premium for each bedroom can make money if it is possible. Worth considering. But they must meet the requirement of legal bedrooms in nyc (which I will not share here because the requirements change often—look it up)

# FOR SELLERS: BEFORE YOU SELL - DETAILS YOUR AGENT NEEDS TO KNOW

There are a few things to get in order before your sale that will allow your agent to create a much slicker presentation of your place which could absolutely lead to greater buyer interest. It's honestly shocking to me how many basic questions about a property even good agents respond to with "I don't know" and then lose buyer interest while they take time to get those answers. Because agents are in the business of pleasing sellers they may feel like 'bothering' you with minutia about your sale could be a turn off and as a result might be ignorant about things they probably should know about when buyers ask.

In addition, while real estate agents are welcome to get answers from your management company—a dirty little secret is that your typical property manager finds real estate agents super annoying. A certain distain towards agents in nyc is kind of the norm. There's a long historical reason for this- mostly that agents offer property managers nothing and often ask for a lot, and sometimes believe their needs should be met immediately regardless of the management company's workload. And as much as agents try to show their best most considerate nature to sellers—they don't always do this with management companies. As a result – agents are expected to limit their questions to management, and in the event that there is confusion at all about the purchase application requirements (there often is) the agent might want to make sure they haven't worn out their welcome before that time.

So, yes, your agent can and should go get answers to questions about your property themselves, it can be more efficient to get the info to them yourself upfront. Your management company will be far more responsive to you – after all you pay them.

1. Make sure your agent has a copy of your offering plan (also known as an offering memorandum – but that term is typically used for new construction). They are going to need to provide it to the buyer's attorney as soon as the contract goes out. In case you don't remember what the offering plan is – it's a very large document – hundreds of pages that you probably received when you purchased your apartment. It includes details about the building and bylaws. If you need to get another copy because you have misplaced it, you might have a neighbor who will allow you to copy theirs, otherwise larger real estate brokerages have limited databases of them, so your agent might be able to retrieve it for you. Otherwise, you can pay your management company to give you a new copy. this might take a week or so.
2. Get a copy of the building's most recent purchase application and current financials from your management company to give to your agent. It is very helpful for them to have the application in advance, in part, because it may give clues to what the board or condo association feels is important in a prospective purchaser, they may answer some questions buyers

will have, plus the financials will be required by the buyer's attorney once the contract is fully executed.
3. If there are any amenities in the building that involve additional fees, find out what they are and let your agent know, and if there is a wait list for those amenities, ask your management company for an estimate of length.
4. Tell your agent about any flip taxes or assessments in the building.
5. If there are any repairs taking place in the building while you are selling ask about what they are if you don't know and try to get an estimate of when they might be completed
6. Share the details of the sublease policy in your building.
7. If there are any terrific, unique, features of either your building or your neighborhood – share them with your agent. (e.g., Doorman is awesome and has been there forever, the best French bakery in NYC is right around the corner, you can see the $4^{th}$ of July fireworks from your apartment or from the roof of your building)
8. If you will need some time, post-closing, to figure out where to go next, or to buy another place, there are a few ways to accomplish this but be aware that most buyers don't love it. In a typical transaction you vacate completely and clean before closing ('broom swept' is the term used) and hand over keys at the closing itself. All neat and clean. However occasionally that is not possible, and arrangements can be made for you to 'rent back' the residence from the new owner for a pre-determined amount of time. This kind od 'lease back' arrangement would need to be worked out ahead of time before contract signing. Let your agent know up front if this is what you are

hoping to do.

# FOR SELLERS: BEFORE YOU SELL – STAGING AND PLANNING TO SHOW

Ah – it's showtime. Selling your place, if you are still living in it, or have a tenant in place is nothing if not disruptive. Not going to lie to you - it is not fun, at all, to show your apartment but with a little advance planning I will offer you here – it can be smoother. But here's the catch – things you can do to improve your sale are in direct opposition to your, or your tenants, personal comfort.

1. Decluttering is always a good idea – but this is really a misnomer. In a typical NYC real estate sale, we are not merely asking you to 'declutter' in a normal way, we are suggesting that you remove two thirds of your belongings from your place until it looks like a showroom for a model home, making living there with any kind of normalcy very challenging.

And yes, I'm afraid this does help sell apartments. In part because having an artificially limited amount of stuff makes any space look larger but also because buyers don't want to see your stuff while they are trying to imagine *their* stuff in that space. Yes, even furniture that is a normal part of your life might benefit your sale by disappearing. Replacing a large dining table with a tiny one for instance is a common staging trick—and in fact I often caution buyers to confirm that there is *any* place to eat a meal in the staging of an apartment. Too often there is not, and people don't even notice.

This does not mean that no one will buy your apartment if you either won't or can't pare down to nothingness.

If you are unable to pare down to total sparseness, there are a few things you *can* do, in addition to making best use of the spaces no one sees (under the bed… any storage you have etc. etc.). The most important things to stash away are the most personal items. De cluttering serves two purposes, enlarging the space and de personalizing it, so family pictures, any collections, awards, religious symbols, or evidence of children should ideally be hidden before showings. You want buyers to feel like the place belongs to them – not you.

2. Cleaning before showings- I have seen people frantic about cleaning up before showings often causing them a fair bit of stress. As opposed to hiding personal items (which I do actually believe is very important for the sale, perfect cleaning matters less, though, of course, that depends on what 'tidy' means to you. Addressing the basics is good: Make the beds, put away anything on surfaces or on the floor, address any unpleasant odors with spray or ventilation, vacuum and sweep if there is visible mess… clean the toilet if it needs it, but you do NOT need to panic and deep clean the place every time your agent wants to show.

3. Be gone during showings. Yes, it is worth the inconvenience of hiding your family or your tenant in the stairwell again and again so your agent can

show your place in peace. The reason this is so important is for the same reasons as decluttering and depersonalizing... more people in the place naturally makes it feel smaller plus, and more significantly, you are inhibiting your customers ability to imagine they own the place in a more personal way. Having to show around a tenant is *slightly* better than having to show around an owner – but not by much. Do what you must do to incentivize your tenant to get out for showings and not come back until they are over. Offer to pay them if you must.

If, you, or a tenant, *must* be present during a showing please for the love of God, DO NOT SAY ANYTHING to the buyers (and instruct your tenant not to) except maybe a polite greeting as they arrive. Let your agent do the job of selling your place. Trust me – I don't care how amazing you might be at selling other things--- you CAN NOT do as good a job of selling your own apartment as a non-occupant can. No customer will believe any nice things you say—plus, more than once, I have seen owners or tenants inadvertently get talking about their experience living there and share details that are unhelpful to the sale, if not downright detrimental.

4. Staging...To stage or not to stage? Or should you stage virtually'? This topic is so complex – I'm going to keep this section brief because the long version is just too long. There are several options here – a. virtual staging, b. real staging (requires an empty apartment) c. no staging d. a hybrid approach. For the sake of brevity – I generally prefer some kind of hybrid strategy that is based mostly around 'fixing problems' with the existing space. Examples include:

   a. If a bedroom is small but large enough to

accommodate a full-sized bed put a real full-sized bed in it so people can believe it.

b. For an empty apartment I always prefer real staging or even limited real staging over virtual staging… make sure there is a chair or loveseat in the living room so that buyers can sit down if they want to have a seat while they visit. At least one bedroom should have a bed in it—in part just because people have overall very nice associations with beds.

c. Limited virtual staging can be helpful when a place is furnished unattractively or an empty place cannot be staged however, virtual staging can have the same effect as using heavy editing or filters on listing photos—You don't want the buyers initial feeling walking into the place to be disappointment—so it's a delicate balance.

# FOR SELLERS: OFFERS

Ah offers! What a nice feeling when they come in. Your agent is happy. You are happy. If the numbers are what you are looking for - you are nearly done... or are you? Here are a few things to consider as you review offers for your sale.

As weirdly casual as this might seem, for something worth a lot of money it is not uncommon for a buyer's first offer to be submitted in just a brief email, with only their offering price, the percentage down, plus any contingencies (financing or inspection). I try not to submit such sparse offers if I can avoid it – but plenty of buyers (often, better funded ones) will sometimes just refuse to provide details or papers until they do an initial check to see if their offer is even in the ballpark.

Plus there can sometimes be an advantage in submitting faster even without all the backup that will be required later on – while the NYC real estate honor code isn't exactly quaker school level, there is (somewhat sweetly I think) often special consideration of the first offers that come in – and though no part of the transaction is binding until the contract is signed by both sides (weeks later), buyers and sellers alike often show a remarkable amount of restraint and are surprisingly considerate about trying to work with the buyer who's offer has been negotiated first.

Once negotiations get underway there are a few items you are welcome to ask to see if they do not arrive at the time the offer is submitted.

1. *Proof of assets* - If the offer is all cash or even includes a down payment larger than 20% it is reasonable to see a financial statement showing they have the money. Tell them not to be offended – a typical nyc real estate transaction often includes a certain amount of verification of the money people say they have. It's nothing personal. There's just a lot of nonsense out there.

2. *Pre-approval letter* - If they are planning to get financing, they should provide a *very recent* (like within a month or two) pre-approval letter from a bank saying that they will lend the right amount. Even better – ask them to give you a pre-approval letter naming your property. Why? Because occasionally a bank will pre-approve lending for the buyer but will have an issue with the building—this is a great way to discover that upfront. Having said that – if there is something unusual about lending in your building... the bank might come back with a 'maybe' answer until they get responses to a questionnaire that would need to be filled out by the building - which takes a while so you may choose to move forward with negotiations with the presumption that they will get approved ultimately, but at least you will be informed about any prospective issues.

3. *Financial Statement* - There is a form, in addition to the typical offer form, that buyers can submit called a financial statement – it goes into real detail about their assets and liabilities. It is not always provided as part of the initial offer (though I always ask my buyers to fill it out. Sometimes they hate it.) and it's a little bit of a project.

Typically, though, this same form has to be included with the purchase application (or a page provided by the building just like it) so the work they put into it will not be wasted if their offer isn't accepted but as a seller, if you are measuring competing offers, it's really helpful to have. You would immediately know things about the buyers that a typical co-op board would be interested in like how much cash would be in their bank account after the purchase and how much debt they have.

Once you have collected all the paperwork you need to satisfy your curiosity and feel that you and your agent can make an informed decision here are some things you may want to consider as you review offers:

1. How much are they putting down? This matters in a couple of ways. The first is that the more they put down, if they are going to be purchasing with financing, the greater the chance they will get the loan they are applying for, presuming their income justifies that amount (of course, dependent on other details of their financial profile). If you are comparing apples to apples (which, of course you nearly never are) the buyer with the larger down payment is often considered lower risk. Also some buildings require higher down payments than others regardless of the expectations of the bank. These range from 10% to as much as 50% down with 20% being the most common.
2. How committed are they to the purchase? This is a little hard to determine but you are welcome to ask if they have offers in on other places simultaneously but know that they have no obligation to tell you. It

is however worth being aware that *any* offer comes with the risk of pulling out before contract signing and sending you back to the drawing board- so if you or your agent can get any kind of read on the prospective buyers' solidity – it's helpful to know. Plus have your agent keep showing for back up until the contract is signed.
3. For co-op sellers: Will the buyer have enough assets in the bank after the purchase to satisfy your co-op board? If you have not done it already – reach out to your board to determine what kind of 'cash in banks' (also known as 'post close liquidity') they want to see after the sale.

Possible answers to how much they have to be able to show after the sale range from six months of mortgage plus maintenance after the purchase (this is the amount you have to show in liquid after all closing cost expenses are paid) to a year of mortgage and maintenance, to a *whole* lot more than that in very fancy places The post close liquidity requirements sometimes come up as a surprise last minute because buyers are not always aware that even though they may have enough cash to put down to satisfy the bank to receive a mortgage for a certain amount – co-ops generally have higher expectations of liquidity than the bank does. Condos will still sometimes also have requirements of cash after the sale – but they tend to be less stringent.

# FOR BUYERS: BEFORE YOU START LOOKING

If I were interested in buying an apartment and needed financing in NYC the first thing I would do is get pre-approved for a loan. This is a speedy process that takes place over the phone with any bank. They will ask you financial questions and based on your answers they will send you a pre-approval email letting you know how much they think they can realistically lend, and some guess at an interest rate.

None of these details are binding at this point but they are a good start. Most people are surprised by how much money they are approved for – it is typically less, or more, than they anticipate very rarely are peoples estimates of what they can get correct. In any case – it is a logical first step as you plan any purchase so you know how much you can spend. Also, rarely, but occasionally, a listing agent will ask to see this letter in order to set up a showing for you so they don't waste time showing apartments to buyers who can't afford them.

The next thing I would do is give some deep thought to what I wanted to buy and where. Whether you are buying for investment or for your personal use – even the most flexible buyers generally have a list of requirements or preferences they may not even realize they have consciously. In my experience there are several ways to discover what you really want and I suggest you employ all of them because they each offer a different perspective on what is available to you-- getting you to what you want faster.

My first suggestion involves thinking ahead about a broad selection of housing attributes and putting them into your order of preference. I have created an extensive list of possible apartment features that I share with my customers, making it easy for them to consider what their priorities are for their purchase. A pdf version is available for sale for $2.99 on my website at www.floriorealestate.com if you want a copy.

Considering what you are looking for in an organized way, ahead of time, is incredibly helpful –maybe especially if you are purchasing with another person. Arranging the list in order together with your co-purchaser is no easy feat but worth doing so you can get at least *some* of the inevitable debates out of the way ahead of time.

My second suggestion should be obvious but sometimes is not –especially for people moving to nyc from out of town. You MUST know what neighborhoods you might want to purchase in. Please God please do not let another out-of-town purchaser tell me they don't know what neighborhoods they want - or that they are open to anywhere *nice*. Do NOT leave the choice of neighborhood up to your agent even if you think that they and you are in complete alignment about what a *nice* neighborhood entails. There is so much variety in NYC (part of it's charm) that your agent cannot satisfactorily explain areas to you – except in the most basic way as a starting point for your own exploration.

Trying to have your agent sort this out for you generally becomes a time consuming nightmare, and I have never seen it result in a purchase without a lot of wasted time and confusion. Whether or not it is convenient to your schedule—you must come and see the neighborhoods you are considering. NYC isn't as neighborhood specific as, let's say, Chicago – but it's not that different either. Also NYC neighborhoods are often rather large and therefore tend to have sort of *micro neighborhoods* within them. It is not uncommon for a buyer to say they love a certain neighborhood only to discover they *hate* certain blocks of it but love others.

Please come to NYC and walk around the neighborhoods you think you might be interested in. Then narrow down your search to just a few– 4 or 5 max. Your agent cannot do a good job for you if your search area is too large – they just can't, and no amount of description in the world is going to illustrate the reality of a given area sufficiently.

The third thing that will help you, and that there is also no way around, is seeing a number of properties, either in person, or asking your agent to preview them with good quality video or live video tours for the specific purpose of discovering how your budget translates into real live NYC housing reality. Even one weekend out at open houses (typically on Sundays) can often give you a much better perspective on what your dollars will get you, so you can get started on considering what sacrifices you might have to make or how much you might want to increase your budget if you can. In general, buyers are struck very quickly by the hard choices they will have to make once they start to visit actual properties within their anticipated budget.

It is very rare that buyers can have *everything* they want within the money they have available. Even the most affluent buyers are often surprised by what getting *all of* what they want will cost. They will see places that are perfect in every way except they lack light, or they have light, but the rooms all face a wall, or the living room has a nice view but the bedroom faces a wall.

In NYC the housing inventory is so dense that even at higher price points (3m and above) you will still find plenty of wall-facing bedrooms, so everyone at nearly every price point will have some sacrifices to make. Seeing the actual places that you can afford in the neighborhoods you want, sooner than later, will quickly give you a sense of what to expect within your budget.

# FOR BUYERS: BOROUGHS AND NEIGHBORHOODS

The basics: There are 5 Boroughs in NYC.

If you aren't from NYC the notion of Boroughs might be a bit of a mystery to you. If it's any comfort NY natives rarely think about them at all unless it is to determine a train route or for feeing a sense of local pride. Even the word Borough is off-putting. What are Boroughs? They lack the cohesiveness of cities or towns and don't exist in other parts of the country.

Boroughs are somewhat significant in terms of political distribution and data and the districts within them matter in terms of schools and sometimes political representation, but otherwise, they were important roughly a century ago. For these purposes don't worry about them too much, except that you should probably figure out which one you want to purchase in. Once you have figured that out – please, please, please, spend the time to walk around and familiarize yourself with what neighborhoods you might want to live in if you don't know already.

Just FYI these are the boroughs of NYC – there are five:

1. The Bronx

2. Manhattan

3. Brooklyn

4. Queens

5. Staten Island

# BRONX NEIGHBORHOODS:

**West Bronx**

Northwest Bronx

- Bedford Park
- Belmont (Arthur Avenue)
- Fordham
    - Fordham Heights
    - Fordham Manor
- Jerome Park previously the grounds of the Jerome Park Racetrack
- Kingsbridge
    - Kingsbridge Heights
    - Van Cortlandt Village
- Marble Hill (part of Manhattan, but often associated with the Bronx due to its mainland location)
- Norwood
- Riverdale
    - Central Riverdale
    - Fieldston
    - Hudson Hill
    - North Riverdale

- Spuyten Duyvil (South Riverdale)
- University Heights
- Woodlawn Heights (North of Woodlawn Cemetery)

Southwest Bronx ("South Bronx")

- Bathgate
- Claremont
- Concourse
- East Tremont
- Highbridge
- Hunts Point
- Longwood
  - Foxhurst
  - Woodstock
- Melrose
- Morris Heights
- Morrisania
  - Crotona Park East
- Mott Haven
  - Port Morris
- The Hub
- Tremont
  - Fairmount
  - Mount Eden
  - Mount Hope
- West Farms

**East Bronx**

Northeast Bronx

- Allerton
  - Bronxwood
  - Laconia
- Baychester
- Bronxdale
- City Island
- Co-op City
- Eastchester
- Edenwald
- Pelham Gardens
- Pelham Parkway
- Wakefield
  - Washingtonville
- Williamsbridge
  - Olinville

Southeast Bronx

- Bronx River (on the border of East and West)
- Bruckner
- Clason Point
- Country Club
- Harding Park
- Morris Park
  - Indian Village: Indian Village is very small, with only a few streets, including Seminole, Tenbroeck, Hering, Narragansett, Chocktaw, Pelham Parkway South,

Pawnee, Yates, and Van Housen; Rhinelander and Neill near Seminole are also considered part of "Indian Village." Former Senator Guy Velella owned a home off Seminole.

- Parkchester
- Park Versailles
- Pelham Bay
- Soundview
- Schuylerville
- Throggs Neck *(also spelled Throgs Neck)*
    - Edgewater Park
- Unionport
    - Castle Hill
- Van Nest
- Westchester Heights
- Westchester Square

# MANHATTAN NEIGHBORHOODS:

**Upper Manhattan**

- Marble Hill
- Inwood
- Fort George (part of Washington Heights)
- Washington Heights
- Hudson Heights (part of Washington Heights)
- West Harlem
- Hamilton Heights (part Harlem)
- West Harlem
- Hamilton Heights (part of Harlem)
- Manhattanville
- Morningside Heights
- Central Harlem
- Harlem
- St Nicholas Historic District aka 'Strivers Row' (Central Harlem)
- Astor Row (Central Harlem)
- Sugar Hill (Central Harlem)
- Marcus Garvey Park, Mount Morris Historical District

- Le Petit Senegal (Little Senegal)
- East Harlem (Spanish Harlem)
- Upper East Side
- Lenox Hill

**Midtown Neighborhoods**

- Carnegie Hill
- Yorkville
- Upper West Side
- Manhattan Valley
- Lincoln Square (once San Juan Hill)
- Columbus Circle
- Sutton Place
- Rockefeller Center
- Diamond District
- Theater District
- Turtle Bay
- Midtown East
- Midtown
- Tudor City
- Little Brazil
- Times Square
- Hudson Yards
- Midtown West
- Hell's Kitchen
- Garment District
- Herald Square
- Koreatown

- Murray Hill aka Little India (former Little Armenia)
- Tenderloin
- Madison Square

## Between Midtown and Lower Manhattan

- Flower District
- Brookdale
- Hudson Yards
- Kips Bay
- Rose Hill
- NoMad
- Peter Cooper Village (former Gas House District)
- Chelsea
- Flatiron District
- Gramercy Park
- Stuyvesant Town (former Gas House district)
- Meatpacking District
- Waterside Plaza

## Lower Manhattan

- Little Germany (historic)
- Alphabet City ad Loisaida
- East Village
- Greenwich Village
- NoHo
- Bowery
- West Village
- Lower East Side

- Soho
- Nolita (Nolita)
- Little Italy
- Chinatown
- Financial District
- Cooperative Village
- Two Bridges
- Tribeca
- Civic Center
- South Street Seaport Historical District
- Battery Park City

**Islands**

- Ellis Island
- Governors Island
- Liberty Island
- Randalls and Wards Islands
- Roosevelt Island

# BROOKLYN NEIGHBORHOODS:

## Central Brooklyn

- Crown Heights
    - Weeksville
- Flatbush
    - Beverley Squares: Beverley Square East, Beverley Square West
    - Ditmas Park
    - East Flatbush
        - Farragut
        - Remsen Village
    - Fiske Terrace
    - Pigtown
    - Wingate
- Prospect Park area
    - Prospect Lefferts Gardens
    - Prospect Park South
    - Windsor Terrace[1]
- Kensington
    - Ocean Parkway
    - Parkville

## Eastern Brooklyn

- Brownsville
- Canarsie
- East New York
  - City Line
  - Cypress Hills
  - New Lots
  - Spring Creek
  - Starrett City
- Highland Park

## Northern Brooklyn

- Bedford–Stuyvesant[2]
  - Bedford
  - Ocean Hill
  - Stuyvesant Heights
- Bushwick
  - Wyckoff Heights
  - East Williamsburg
- Greenpoint
  - Little Poland
- Williamsburg

## Northwestern Brooklyn

- Brooklyn Heights
- Brooklyn Navy Yard
  - Admiral's Row
- Cadman Plaza
- Clinton Hill

- Downtown Brooklyn
    - Bridge Plaza/RAMBO
- DUMBO
    - Fulton Ferry
- Fort Greene
- Prospect Heights
    - Pacific Park/Atlantic Yards
- Vinegar Hill
- South Brooklyn – takes its name from the geographical position of the original town of Brooklyn, which today includes the neighborhoods listed above under the heading "northwestern Brooklyn." It is not located in the southern part of the modern borough.
    - Boerum Hill
    - Carroll Gardens
    - Columbia Street Waterfront District
    - Cobble Hill
    - Gowanus
    - Park Slope
    - <u>Park Slope South</u>
    - <u>Greenwood Heights</u>
    - Red Hook

## Southern Brooklyn

- Barren Island
- Bergen Beach and Georgetown
- Coney Isalnd
- Brighton Beach, also known as

"Little Odessa"[3] or "Little Russia"[4]
- West Brighton
  - Manhattan Beach
  - Sea Gate
- Sheepshead Bay and Madison
  - Homecrest
- Midwood
- Flatlands
- Gerritsen Beach
- Gravesend
  - White Sands
- Marine Park
- Mill Basin
- Plumb Beach

## Southwestern Brooklyn

The southwestern portion of Brooklyn shares numbered streets and avenues starting from 36th Street to 101st Street and from 1st Avenue to 25th Avenue, passing through the neighborhoods listed below, respectively.

- Bay Ridge
  - Fort Hamilton
- Bensonhurst
  - Bath Beach
  - New Utrecht
- Borough Park
  - Mapleton which lies mostly in Borough Park but its southern reaches are within Bensonhurst

- Dyker Heights
- Sunset Park
  - Chinatown
  - Sunset Industrial Park

# QUEENS NEIGHBORHOODS:

**Northwestern Queens**

- Astoria
  - Astoria Heights
  - Ditmars
    - Steinway
  - Little Egypt
- Jackson Heights
- Long Island City
  - Blissville
  - Hunters Point
  - Dutch Kills
  - Queensbridge (housing development)
  - Queensview (housing development)
  - Queens West
  - Ravenswood (housing development)
- Sunnyside
  - Sunnyside Gardens
- Woodside

## Southwestern Queens

- The Hole
- Howard Beach
  - Hamilton Beach
  - Howard Park
  - Lindenwood (housing development)
  - Old Howard Beach
  - Ramblersville
  - Rockwood Park
- Ozone Park
  - South Ozone Park
  - Tudor Village
- Richmond Hill
- Woodhaven

## Central Queens

- Briarwood
- Corona
  - LeFrak City (housing development)
  - North Corona
- East Elmhurst
- Elmhurst
- Forest Hills
  - Forest Hills Gardens
- Fresh Pond
- Glendale
- Jackson Heights

- Kew Gardens
- Maspeth
- Middle Village
- Rego Park
- Ridgewood
  - Wyckoff Heights

**Northeastern Queens**

- Bayside
  - Bay Terrace
  - Bayside Hills
  - Fort Totten
  - Oakland Gardens
- Bellerose
- College Point
- Douglaston–Little Neck
  - Douglaston
    - Douglas Bay
    - Douglas Manor
    - Douglaston Hill
    - Douglaston Park
    - Winchester Estates
  - Little Neck
    - Pines
    - Little Neck Hills
    - Westmoreland
- Flushing
  - Broadway-Flushing
  - Bowne Park

- Chinatown
- Downtown Flushing
- Koreatown
- Linden Hill
- Murray Hill
- Willets Point
- Pomonok
- Electchester
- Queensboro Hill
- Floral Park
- Auburndale
- Kew Gardens Hills
- Fresh Meadows
  - Hillcrest
  - Utopia
- Glen Oaks
  - North Shore Towers (housing development)
- Whitestone
  - Beechhurst
  - Clearview
  - Malba

## Southeastern Queens

- Bellaire
- Brookville
- Cambria Heights
- Hollis
  - Hollis Hills

- Jamaica
    - Holliswood
    - Jamaica Estates
    - Jamaica Hills
    - South Jamaica
    - Rochdale Village (Cooperative Housing Development)
    - St. Albans
- Laurelton
- Meadowmere
- Queens Village
- Rosedale
- Springfield Gardens
- Warnerville

## The Rockaways

- Arverne
- Bayswater
- Belle Harbor
- Breezy Point
- Broad Channel
- Edgemere
- Far Rockaway
- Hammels
- Neponsit
- Rockaway Beach
- Rockaway Park
- Roxbury

ALEXANDRA FLORIO

- Seaside

# STATEN ISLAND NEIGHBORHOODS:

North Shore
(Community District 1)

Arlington
Northern Castleton Corners
Clifton
Concord
Elm Park

Fort Wadsworth
Northern Graniteville

Grymes Hill
Livingston
Mariners Harbor
Northern Meiers Corners
New Brighton
Port Ivory
Port Richmond
Randall Manor
Rosebank
Saint George
Shore Acres
Silver Lake
Stapleton
Sunnyside

ALEXANDRA FLORIO

Tompkinsville
West-New-Brighton
Westerleigh

Mid-Island
(Community District 2)
- Arrochar
- Bloomfield
- Bulls Head
- Southern Castleton Corners
- Chelsea
- Dongan Hills
- Egbertville
- Emerson Hill
- Southern Graniteville
- Grant City
- Grasmere
- Heartland Village
- Midland Beach
- New Dorp
- New Springville
- Oakwood
- Ocean Breeze
- Old Town
- Richmondtown
- South Beach
- Todt Hill
- Travis
- Southern Willowbrook

South Shore
(Community District 3)
    Bay Terrace
    Brighton Heights
    Charleston
    Eltingville
    Great Kills
    Greenridge
    Huguenot
    Lighthouse Hill
    Manor Heights
    Meiers Corners
    Old Place
    Park Hill
    Pleasant Plains
    Prince's Bay
    Richmond Valley
    Rossville
    Sandy Ground
    Stapleton Heights
    Teleport
    Tottenville
    Ward Hill
    Woodrow

Related Areas
    West Shore

Annadale
Arden Heights

East Shore

# FOR BUYERS: WHERE TO LOOK FOR LISTINGS IN NYC

There are really only two worthwhile ways to list your place or search for housing in NYC. Either **through listings sent directly to you by a real estate agent you trust** from their company's internal search system, or on your own through **Streeteasy**. Yes, there are plenty of alternative real estate search sites available which work fine in other parts of the country, Zillow, Realtor, etc.... but they are, at best, redundant in NYC, at worst, littered with expired listings left online as bait-and-switch by agents hoping to gain customers. Just skip them. They will only confuse you and falsely lead you to believe there are terrific listings out there that your agent is failing to send you.

I have had customers ask me what places *I have*, as in mine proprietarily, and sure, I would love it if you bought one of the listings I have been contracted to sell but, in general, when an agent sends you residences, they should include not only whatever places they themselves are selling, but every listing that matches your criteria for sale anywhere throughout NYC-- by any agency. If you notice that your agent is disproportionately sending listings from their own company or with them as the listing agent, you might want to ask them about this. It would be unusual and could mean they are promoting their own listings where they claim full commission, as opposed to the complete range of listings from every agency, where they would be acting as your buyer's agent but not the listing agent, and therefore only be entitled to half.

# FOR BUYERS: STEPS TO PURCHASING

The typical purchasing process, with financing, takes roughly 8-12 weeks depending on the property type and the details of the loan.

- A. Mortgage Preapproval (if financing) and Property Search
- B. Offer preparation.
- C. Offer Negotiation and Acceptance
- D. Contract Review/ Attorney Due Diligence
- E. Buyer signs contract & escrow deposit
- F. Seller signs contract & sends copy to buyer
- G. Loan application & appraisal
- H. Loan approval and commitment letter issued from bank
- I. Co-op Board Package and Interview/ Condo Application (scheduling board interview may take 2-3 weeks after application is submitted)
- J. Bank & Attorney Prepare for Closing
- K. Bank Gives Clearance to Close
- L. Closing Scheduled
- M. Final Walk-through & Closing

# FOR BUYERS: CO-OPS VS CONDOS

The experience of living in a co-op instead of a condo is very similar but the ownership and rules can often be quite different. Technically, when you purchase a co-op you are buying shares in the ownership interest of the building--like shares in a corporation, whereas for a condo – the units are sold independently. You own the unit itself, and the common spaces are owned by the condo association, and building taxes are paid separately. When you purchase a condo you receive a *deed* like when you buy a house whereas with a co-op you receive what is known as a *proprietary lease*.

Outline of differences:
1. Co-ops represent the monthly costs of ownership as one number called 'maintenance' This number includes common charges and your units share of property tax. Condos generally represent monthly charges as two separate numbers, 'common charges' and 'taxes'.
2. Co-ops typically have some restrictions about subleasing – Here are some possibilities:
    a. Require owner occupancy for a certain number of years… ranging from one to three before you are allowed to sublease.

      b. Allowed to sublease for a limited number of years before you must return to occupy the apartment

      c. Only a certain number of units can be subleased at one time within the building. Generally, in single digits.

3. Condos will always allow you to sublease from day one.
4. Both condos and co-ops typically require that you have any prospective tenants complete an application and submit it to the Condo Association or Co-op Board for review and approval. The co-op approval process and screening can generally be longer and more extensive than for condos.
5. Co-ops can choose to either self-manage or hire a management company. Condos always have an outside management company. Smaller co-ops sometimes even allocate building chores to individual owners on a voluntary or rotating basis but there is huge variation in this. The only way to know is to ask how the building is managed.
6. The cost per square foot is typically higher in condos than co-ops – they are desirable to investors because of the immediate ability to sublease and the straightforward ownership relationship and so you may find yourself competing with investors who frequently make cash offers more often when purchasing a condo.
7. Another distinction is that despite higher price points condos generally have more liberal financing requirements. Typically, condos require only 10 percent down and have less strict requirements for cash after the sale... whereas most co-ops require 20 percent down and will ask for demonstration of upwards of 6 months of mortgage and maintenance payments in the bank after all closing costs are paid.

8. Closing costs for condos are typically higher than for comparable condos.

# FOR BUYERS: GETTING A LOAN

The majority of buyers need financing-- though it is helpful to know that in a competitive bidding situation, offers that do *not* require a loan have an advantage. It is also possible to make an offer with the intention to finance but *without* a 'mortgage contingency'. In this case you agree to be contractually committed to pay in cash in the event your loan does not pan out – proof of assets (a bank statement showing you have the offering price in cash) would be required at the time of the offer just like in a cash-only purchase.

The reason sellers have a preference for all cash is that it assures the fastest and most secure sale. With any loan there is always some risk of things falling through. In addition, purchasing with a loan typically requires a two or three months' waiting period while financing is secured. But let's presume you are in the vast majority of buyers that need or want financing. Determining the amount you can borrow (getting pre-approved) should ideally happen even before you start looking for a place to buy.

The first step is to contact any bank (don't worry too much at this point about which bank that is – you are in no way committed to applying for financing with the first lending institution you call) in order to have a roughly half an hour conversation allowing them to 'pre-approve' you. They will ask you about your income, how much cash you have in the bank, any debt you are carrying, and any assets you might have, plus other details relevant to your financial picture. After this conversation they will email you what is known a 'pre-approval' letter with a maximum dollar amount on it that they are offering to lend. The number in this letter is often a surprise to buyers – even ones who are confident about the amount they will be able to borrow. Most buyers discover that the amount they are pre-qualified for is either a fair bit higher or lower than they had imagined. In any case it's really good to know how much you have got before you go shopping.

Another reason to get pre-approved before starting to look is that some selling agents may require a copy of that letter in order to be willing to arrange a showing for you. They figure that if you can't afford the place there's no point in showing it. Your pre-approval letter will be all you need until you find the place you want- have your offer accepted- and the contract is signed.

I have though, worked with customers who have gone through the whole process of providing all paperwork to the lender for the secondary step in getting a loan, and receive what is known as a 'commitment letter' even before they have found a property to offer on. This is very uncommon, but I don't understand why. It makes sellers much more comfortable to see that the buyers have gone through the extra steps for approval, and it certainly gives you an advantage over buyers without a commitment. If you can I urge you to consider doing it.

Typically, though – you complete your loan application *after* you are in contract. Providing the financial materials necessary to receive a commitment letter is time consuming but if you are purchasing a co-op -- the board application will use a lot of the same paperwork. It's standard financial stuff like tax returns and pay stubs.


As you are gathering financial materials to give to your lender the bank will simultaneously be reviewing details of the building you want to buy into --to determine that they are willing to lend within it. There are two parts to final loan approval - the you part and your credit worthiness, and the building part.

The review of the building generally includes a questionnaire to be filled out by the management company asking about percentages of owner occupancy ( many subleased units in a building are considered a greater risk than mostly owner occupied), number of sponsor units (units owned by the building), how many owners in total there are in the building, and whether or not a substantial number of units are owned by one entity (considered higher risk if one owner holds a lot of units), the financial health of the building overall, its general condition, and what kind of insurance policy it carries. The bank will also arrange for an independent appraisal to be done of the unit you are considering.

Presuming the building is determined to be warrantable (deserving of a loan) the bank will issue you a 'commitment letter' which outlines the final terms of your mortgage - and then you are in the home stretch. Once the much-anticipated letter is provided to you, something that can be slightly confusing, is that the first version you will receive often includes a number of 'conditions' that will have to be met in order to satisfy the terms of the loan- so you aren't really done yet – but you are close.

Because your commitment letter needs to be included with your board application, you now need to determine whether a commitment letter with *any* conditions will be acceptable to include, and if so, what conditions will be allowed. The application may specify that the building requires a commitment completely free of conditions—but if it is not clear- the only way to find out is to ask the management company (or have your agent ask).

It is also likely that your board application will require that you include further proof that you have received the loan in the form of something called Aztech agreements. These will often come to you in triplicate by mail and assure that you will be provided with the financing you seek at the rate you expect given the completion of the conditions of the commitment letter.

Hold on to these forms, sign them each, and then you will probably provide them to the building along with your application. If they are not requested as part of your package just hang onto them until the closing. You will need to bring them along or may be asked for them by either your broker, attorney, or lender prior. Just don't misplace them. They matter.

Ultimately, once all the conditions of your commitment are met and you arrive at the closing table ready with all your checks in hand (as specified ahead of time by your attorney), representatives from both the sellers' bank and your own will meet there to make sure the details of your loan are finalized correctly, and the payoff of the seller's loan is accomplished.

# FOR BUYERS: HOW TO DECIDE HOW MUCH TO OFFER AND HOW HIGH TO GO

There's a certain truth to the idea that a residence is worth, essentially, whatever folks are willing to pay for it. This may be especially true in a market that changes as rapidly as nyc does. That's not to say that comparative properties don't matter just that, really, if a place is getting a lot of interest all around one price it's pretty fair to say that it's "worth" that amount.

The primary way to determine an appropriate offering price for a property is to look at the prices of places with similar features in the immediate area, called 'comps' or 'comparable' properties. My advice is that when you or your agent do this – that you look most carefully at apartments that have been sold recently, not one's that are currently for sale, so that you know that the prices you are comparing are the *actual* sale prices instead of pre-negotiated numbers. The trouble, of course, with finding comparable properties is that it's not uncommon for there to have been very few recent sales in the immediate area that count as comps—plus the variety of features from one place to another is vast and so determining what are actually comparable properties is kind of hard-but still valuable.

Over more than a decade I have learned to create a kind of equation of possible features or deficits in my head, adding and subtracting apartment traits to determine equivalent properties and that works well. But for someone new at this it is a complicated exercise. My advice is that you start by looking at units in the building you are interested in, or as close as possible, using the most basic measurement; square footage, and determining a price per square foot. Then adjust up or down as you add features like 'nice views' or 'good light' 'more recent renovation' and subtract features like 'far from train' or 'high common charges'.

The best advice I have heard for sellers and buyers in determining the *right t*op price during a negotiation, presuming you have started out with numbers that approximate fair market value, is that the price you and the seller agree to should make you *both* feel like you are both being slightly taken advantage of in the transaction. But only slightly.

The other piece of guidance I have given buyers is that in a heated negotiation if you are being pushed by either an assertive seller, or other bidders – stop at the point where you would be upset if they accepted your offer. Or conversely increase your offer if you would be upset if you lost it for a thousand dollars more (this second measure is a little unreliable because there is a reality to how much a place is actually worth and fear of loss might lead you to overpay in a way that could make it hard to resell-but obviously none of these suggestions are a substitute for doing the homework of properly assessing the value at the time of your offer).

# FOR BUYERS: SETTLING IN

To me there is no more exciting or optimistic feeling than getting keys to a new place and eating pizza out of the box on the bare floor as you investigate every knob and outlet you now own. But I also know that not everyone loves that feeling – for some the idea of moving and reorienting to a new location fills them with nostalgia and worry.

For people I have worked with who feel that way, two pieces of advice. 1. It's completely normal to feel sad about leaving your old place but, in my experience, that feeling always goes away once you settle in. It can't feel like home yet if you have never lived there and I have never seen anyone unable to adapt to a new place to live. 2. Even though buying and moving is a headache and can be very expensive, if you have been careful with your purchase and have not massively overpaid. In NYC there is a very good chance that, if, in a couple of years you determine that you would rather be somewhere else – you can sell and move and break even or better. It is rare to ever be truly stuck with New York City real estate unless you have paid a massively inflated price, and even then,N sometimes it still works out.

Things that I know have helped buyers feel at home in a new place:

1.Walk the neighborhood – explore every resource within a 5 block radius. Make note of closing and opening times. One of the more wonderful things about NYC is that most 'micro neighborhoods' often have a solution to nearly every problem. If there is no supermarket nearby it is likely that your local deli may have an 'enhanced' supply of grocery items. Despite how large New York is, most people like to be able to exist entirely in their neighborhood for necessities.

2. Download apps that may help you orient yourself. Citymapper.com is fantastic for directions and the only map and transit program I ever need in NYC, Nextdoor.com offers local info and a chance to talk to neighbors about community concerns, as do community groups on Reddit. Patch.com offers great access to local, more traditional, journalistic news stories, Citizen.com is an app that is crime specific, though personally I found the incessant alerts about neighbors smelling smoke or couples arguing on the sidewalk stressed me out more than it was worth –but it has real value when you can hear a ton of firetrucks and really want to know they aren't heading to your building.

3. Check out food delivery apps. For me, nothing increases my excitement about a new area as seeing all the superb new food I can order there.

4. If you have a little free time – consider volunteering in your new neighborhood. Nothing makes people want to help you get oriented more than the idea that you are interested in giving back.

# ABOUT THE AUTHOR:

Alexandra Florio was born on the Upper West Side and attended PS6 and Hunter College H.S. on the Upper East Side. She received dual BAs in Political Science and Anthropology from Wellesley College and is a 25 year resident of Brooklyn, providing unique opportunities on both sides of the bridge. She has a deep love for the city of New York "It has history, charm, and optimism—an enviable combination for any city". Using street smarts, up-to-the-minute information, and critical analysis, Alexandra Florio has consistently offered impressive and measurable results to both her buyers and sellers over the years and provides flat fee consulting services for newer agents, buyers, and sellers offering an experienced objective view and expertise by phone or in person.

www.ingramcontent.com/pod-product-compliance
Lightning Source LLC
Chambersburg PA
CBHW020433220526
45464CB00002B/687